Tennessee Triumph Cookbook

Celebrating 100 Years of Suffrage 1920 – 2020

Sango FCE
Clarksville-Montgomery County, Tennessee

Produced to help fund
Tennessee Triumph,
the statue
honoring our local Suffragists
Sango Family and Community Educators
2020 Vision Committee
Clarksville, Montgomery County, Tennessee
All Volunteer Effort

Table of Contents

WHY A COOK BOOK?

(L to R) Seated: Barbara Brown Beeman & Pamela Albaro; Standing Brenda Harper & Pat Woods

OH, MY, WHY A COOKBOOK?

In 1886, *The Women Suffrage Cookbook* was compiled by Hattie A. Burr, with recipes from many elite women of the time. Cookbooks of the past are more than recipes; they are histories of Churches, Communities and Civic Organizations. This one can also be a record of involvement in the 2020 Vision Celebration of 100th Anniversary of Suffrage and all the shoulders on which we stand.

"There is a new twist to this fundraiser. No need to burn your fingers or dirty a mixing bowl. Contributors were invited to calculate what it would cost to prepare a favorite recipe and double that amount as the donation for each recipe contributed. Example: Ingredients for Apple Pecan Pie cost $7.50, double that amount would be a $15 donation. Contributors also had the opportunity to write a short statement about the person associated with the recipe," by M. Pile.

All proceeds from the contributions to and the purchases of the cookbook go to fund the Tennessee Triumph Statue, a project spearheaded by Clarksville-Montgomery County Arts and Heritage Development Council Director Ellen Kanervo.

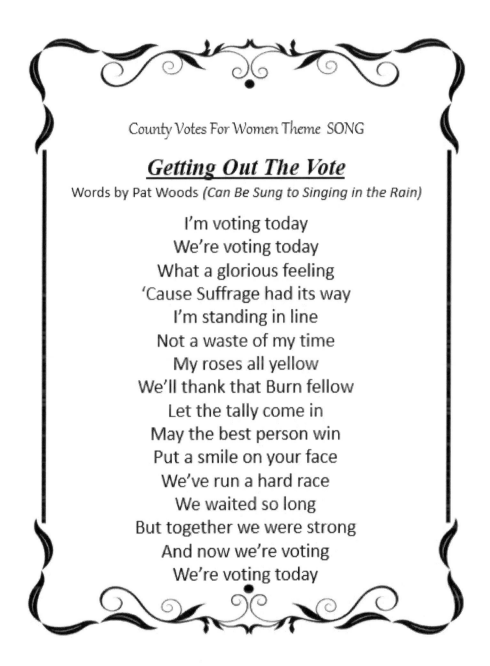

County Votes For Women Theme SONG

Getting Out The Vote

Words by Pat Woods *(Can Be Sung to Singing in the Rain)*

I'm voting today
We're voting today
What a glorious feeling
'Cause Suffrage had its way
I'm standing in line
Not a waste of my time
My roses all yellow
We'll thank that Burn fellow
Let the tally come in
May the best person win
Put a smile on your face
We've run a hard race
We waited so long
But together we were strong
And now we're voting
We're voting today

Smith Trahern Mansion
(Home of Family and Community Education)

The History of Votes For Women Celebration

We are counting down with 2020 Vision to the 100th Celebration of Women's Vote. It began at a convention to advance the legal rights of women held at the Wesleyan Chapel in Seneca Falls, New York, on July 19, 1848. This event was going on a few short years before the Mansion was being built.

Tennessee was The Perfect 36 in 1920, the essential last state that could ratify the 19th Amendment before time ran out! The War of the Roses was between those for and against suffrage. As early as 1867, suffragists adopted yellow to symbolize courage. In the summer of 1920, they wore and distributed yellow roses; the anti-suffragist, red roses. Our thanks to the dedicated activists and to the legislators who voted to ratify.

On August 18th the house passed ratification by one vote when Harry Burn of McMinn County switched sides after receiving a letter from his mother "Hurrah and vote for suffrage...."

The Suffrage Amendment was certified by the U.S. Secretary of State on August 26, 1920, fully enfranchising women across the nation, 72 years after Seneca Falls. In 1971, August 26th was designated as the day to celebrate the Anniversary of **Votes for Women**.

In preparation for the 100th celebration, we started with communication among wide and expanded groups of women and right-thinking men to join us in gathering ideas. Friends of Smith Trahern Mansion celebrated the 75th and the 90th Anniversary and are faithful to the project.

V
OT
E S
F O R
WOMEN
2020 VISION
CELEBRATION
100 YEAR ANNIVERSARY

2020 Vision Committee was created to Celebrate the 100th Year of Votes for Women. We celebrated the 75th and the 90th. In preparation for this celebration, a committee was created in January 2015 that included Debby Johnson, Mansion Director, Martha Pile, Extension Agent and Elizabeth Black, County Communications Director. The first meeting announced and open to all interested people was held in June of 2015. When Elizabeth became Administrator of Elections, Michelle Newell, County Communications Director, and Heather Fleming, City Representative, were added to the committee in her stead. 2020 Vision continues to be open to participation by all who are interested.

Commemorating Clarksville's Suffragists
1920 – 2020

<u>19th Amendment to the United States Constitution</u>

The right of citizens of the United States to vote shall not be denied or abridged by the United States or by any State on account of sex.

Congress shall have power to enforce this article by appropriate legislation.

We are grateful.

"The young women of today - free to study, to speak, to write, to choose their occupation - should remember that every inch of this freedom was bought for them at a great price... the debt that each generation owes to the past, it must pay to the future."

Abigail Scott Duniway

Finding Our History

The 100th anniversary of 19th Amendment ratification, which made Woman Suffrage a Constitutional right nation-wide, takes place in 2020. Thirty-six States were needed to ratify; Tennessee has a special role in that accomplishment as the 36th State to do so.

The 2020 Vision Committee was formed in Montgomery County in 2015 to begin an awareness campaign in anticipation of the anniversary and to encourage its commemoration. As enthusiasm built, interest grew in what had gone on in Clarksville during the years of the Suffrage Movement. Our first clue was a photograph:

Photograph courtesy of Montgomery County Archives

The woman on the right, holding the banner is Constance Rudolph, the only person pictured who had been identified. There was no information about the event, when or where it was taken.

Our first effort was to circulate the photograph, expecting that people would recognize the location and some of the individuals pictured. We put it in print and digital newspapers, on Facebook, on web sites and even printed book marks and distributed them freely. Results were non-existent. No one recognized anyone. Despite the fact that it hangs in the County Court House, some began to wonder whether perhaps it had nothing to do with Clarksville. Did we even know where this photograph originated?

Thanks to Cleo Hogan, local historian and attorney whose family farm neighbored the farm of Constance Rudolph's parents, we were able to make contact with her niece in Oklahoma. Not only did she confirm the identity of her Aunt Constance, but also reported that she had given that photograph of her aunt to our first County Historian, Ursula Smith Beach. Identity and provenance successfully confirmed! But we were no closer to finding our local Suffrage history than when we began.

We next consulted all the resources we could think of that would have relevant records: books, vertical files, documents, manuscripts, diaries, letters, and photographs in area libraries, archives and museums. The Suffrage history we did find had barely a whisper about Clarksville.

The Montgomery County Historical Society website supplied an informative article by County Historian Eleanor Williams. It provided valuable details and confirmed the existence of a local Suffrage organization. But where was the rest of the story hiding?

We concluded that there was one place left to look, *The Clarksville Leaf-Chronicle*. The local newspapers have created a remarkably complete series of reported history for our area. We knew that our Public Library had microfilm of all the available newspaper issues.

Unfortunately, they had never been digitized or indexed other than the obituaries and death notices. The only way to find what was recorded there was to read the microfilm, miles and miles of microfilm.

We used the *Nashville Tennessean* which has been digitized and is ocr-searchable to find any reports of Clarksville Suffrage activities reported there. Just a few lines about a meeting that was held on the lawn at the W. W. Barksdale residence on July 31, 1914 gave us a starting point. That inspired great hope since we knew he was the owner, editor and publisher of the Clarksville newspaper. Our hope was rewarded with a large front page article which recounted a successful and well-attended meeting in great detail.

We then set a goal to scan the Clarksville paper from July 1914 through August 1920 and extract any reports of Suffrage activity. We needed to complete as much as possible within just a few months to make an assessment about our local Suffrage legacy and know whether it warranted erecting a statue in Clarksville as part of the *Tennessee Woman Suffrage Heritage Trail* project.

Our answer was a resounding YES.

We have not yet completed the entire six years and would welcome more volunteers. And we have learned that we need to go well past August 1920 because the story doesn't end there.

As for that original photograph, we still do not know the identity of everyone, but we do know what they were doing that day and where and when it was taken!

Equal Suffrage Meeting A Pronounced Success

Attended by Nearly One Hundred of Our Representative Women and Men —The Address of Mrs. Wallis the Feature of an Interesting Occasion.

Clarksville Leaf-Chronicle August 1, 1914

Clarksville's Woman Suffrage History
Rediscovery of the women in the records...

Lula Poindexter Anderson
Ethel Wilder Bailey
Wilhelmina Barksdale*
Jessie Couts Beach
Katherine Hoey Boillin
Sallie Atkins Bryan*
Margaret Wilkerson Crouch
Mildred Crouch Savage
Lois Townsend Cunningham
Willie Erwin Daniel
Ethel Collier Dickson
Katherine Ireys Diehl*
Maria Stacker Ellis
Lulu Bringhurst Epperson*
Bennie Gill Fort
Petinka Bailey Foskett
Mary Hunt Marks Gholson
Fannie Miller Hodgson
Carrie Johnson
Emma Polk LaPrade*

Emma Higgins Lupton*
Lucy Underwood Meriwether
Stella Thayer Morgan*
Mamie Morris Green Patch
Sallie Hurst Peay
Pearl Darnell Perkins
Olivia Blackman Pickering*
Irene Rollow Polk
Lou Redd Roach*
Constance Rudolph
Florence McKee Rudolph
Frances Pollard Rudolph
Mary Enola Rudolph
Brenda Vineyard Runyon
Corinne Northington Smith
Grace Pratt Stacker
Daisy Neblett Vaughn
Carrie Wallace Wilson
Annie Mimms Winn
*biography follows

So far, we have found 39 women named in the written records. We know there were 65 members of the local Suffrage League in 1919, so there are many others yet to discover.

In addition, we have found strong indicators that local African-American women were Suffrage advocates, even though not yet found in the records surveyed. Research efforts to identify them and their activities continue. Ella Roberts and Emma Burt are two community activists that we think likely to have supported Woman Suffrage.

Portrait Gallery

Minnie Barksdale

Brenda Runyon

Emma Lupton

Sallie Hurst Peay

Portrait   Gallery

Mamie Green Patch

Lucy Meriwether

Mary Marks Gholson

Ethel Collier Dickson

Portrait Gallery

Lois Cunningham

Constance Rudolph

**Petinka BaileyFoskett
(in costume)**

Portrait Gallery

Lulu Bringhurst Epperson

Irene Rollow Hicks

Willie Erwin Daniel

Grace Pratt Stacker

Biographies

We have compiled sufficient information on 9 of the Clarksville Suffragists to write brief biographies and submit them to the *Online Biographical Dictionary of Woman Suffrage in the United States.*

Wilhelmina Sickenberger Barksdale

Host of 1914 open Suffrage meeting in Clarksville, TN; publisher, owner and editor of Clarksville Leaf-Chronicle and The Clarksville Star

Wilhelmina "Minnie" Sickenberger was born August 1, 1867 to Katherina Gaylor and Louis Sickenberger in Evansville, Indiana. A German language teacher, she married William Wallace Barksdale there December 26, 1893. They relocated to Clarksville, Tennessee soon afterwards and lived there the rest of their lives, Minnie until her death January 30, 1954 at age 86.

Minnie Barksdale became actively involved in the Clarksville community as shown by her representing the Wednesday Club in the Federation of Women's Clubs when it was formed to support a building for the Public Library in 1901. The clubs that made up the Federation were social, but also much more. They offered extensive opportunities for their members to study diverse topics of international culture, social issues, gardening, history, art, music, etc.

Her only child, William W. Barksdale, Jr. who later became city mayor, was born in 1912. The family had moved into their 1128 Madison Street home by July 31, 1914 when she hosted the first open meeting of the Clarksville Equal Suffrage League. The 40 member group had organized and elected officers on June 27.

A notice in the local paper invited members of local women's clubs and their husbands to the meeting. The presence of officers from suffrage organizations as distant as New Orleans and Houston, Texas indicates the level of investment and planning. That it was held on the lawn suggests that a large number of attendees were expected.

The front page headline of "Equal Suffrage Meeting a Pronounced Success" in the *Clarksville Leaf-Chronicle* on August 1, 1914 was followed by extensive coverage of the meeting's speeches and the report that between 75 and 80 had attended.

It is not surprising that news of the meeting received such prominent attention in the local newspaper given that W. W. Barksdale was the editor and publisher. The fact that Minnie Barksdale was an active and able partner in the operation of the paper was well-known and evidenced by the consistent, frequent reporting of suffrage news and events from all over the country year after year.

With her husband's sudden death in 1922, Minnie Barksdale assumed his role as editor and publisher of the *Clarksville Leaf Chronicle*. She announced her position on the front page March 13, 1922: "I shall do my utmost to continue the policies of the paper as here-to-fore; to make it the mouthpiece of every clean forward movement; to make it the rallying point for the hosts of progress in the life of the city, country, the state and nation."

Later that same year she was elected to the Board of Directors of the Southern Newspaper Publishers Association. Forced into temporary retirement by ill health, she sold the *Leaf-Chronicle* in 1924, but returned to newspaper publishing in 1934 founding *The Clarksville Star* and operating it with her son until 1940.

By Brenda Harper, volunteer researcher, 2020 Vision Committee, Clarksville, TN

Sallie Atkins Bryan

Treasurer of the Clarksville Equal Suffrage League 1917 and 1918

Sallie Barker Atkins was born in Clarksville, Tennessee to Caroline Barker and George S. Atkins December 25, 1862, but lost her father at an early age. After marrying Henry E. Bryan July 21, 1883 she settled into the rural Hampton Station area of Montgomery County and lived there until her death July 10, 1924. She and her husband reared two adopted children, Fletcher and Lucy Beaumont, from their early childhood.

Sallie Bryan was an early member of the Clarksville Equal Suffrage League and served as its Treasurer in both 1917 and 1918. At the February 26, 1918 meeting where members voted to endorse Mrs. Leslie Warner of Nashville for state president, Sallie collected the dues needed to ensure the local league's representation at the upcoming Memphis meeting where both suffrage organizations were expected to merge.

By Brenda Harper, volunteer researcher, 2020 Vision Committee, Clarksville, TN

Katherine Ireys Diehl

'

Secretary, Clarksville Equal Suffrage League; Ratification Committee, Clarksville League of Women Voters

Katherine Ireys was born January 16, 1878 in Mississippi to Susan and Henry T. Ireys. She had completed one year of college and made her way to Washington, D.C when she met and married Charles E. Diehl there on March 24, 1909.

By the time of the 1910 Federal Census they were living in Clarksville, TN where Charles was the minister of First Presbyterian Church. In October of that same year, their only child Charles Ireys Diehl was born. In later years Charles Diehl became President of Southwestern Presbyterian University. When SPU relocated from Clarksville to Memphis in 1925, the Diehl family went also. Katherine lived there until her death June 19, 1955.

While in Clarksville, Katherine Diehl was a member of the Clarksville Equal Suffrage League. She served as Secretary beginning in 1914. She was an active member when the group transitioned to the League of Women Voters following the passage of the State suffrage law in 1919. She was on the Ratification Committee and help plan the event when Gov. Roberts visited Clarksville in July 1920 and the League held a reception for him at the Women's Club to show support and urge him on toward the ratification of the Federal Amendment.

By Brenda Harper, volunteer researcher, 2020 Vision Committee, Clarksville, TN

Mary Lulu Bringhurst Epperson

Women's Democratic Chair, first woman TN State Librarian, first depositor in world's first women's bank, first woman in Clarksville to own and operate a hotel, among the first women to run an insurance business; Chair of Clarksville area Woman Voters League; attended and served on committees at the Nashville Woman Voters Conference.

Mary Lulu Bringhurst was born in 1870 in Clarksville, Tennessee to William Rufus and Sallie Scott Bringhurst. She married William P. Epperson in 1888 and had a son William, Jr. 1892-1897 and a daughter Sarah Scott Epperson (McGehee) 1893-1976. Lulu's husband died in 1900 and she married her Nashville lawyer, Moreau Pinckney Estes, 1876-1940, son of Judge Joe Henry Estes. They had a daughter, Clara Clark Epperson (Lulu had kept her first husband's name after her marriage to Estes and so the daughter had his name). They later divorced.

In 1901 Lulu was selected to serve as Tennessee's first female State Librarian; her term ran until 1903. Articles praising her contributions to the State Library were included in several publications. In March of 1903, while living in Nashville, she was appointed as agent of the United States Fire Insurance Company of New York. She and her partner, Mollie Claiborne, ran the company as Mrs. Lulu Epperson & Co.

In October of 1908, Lulu alleged that the male-operated insurance agencies in Nashville had illegally banded together to destroy her company. Lulu requested an investigation from Insurance Commissioner Reau E. Folk to see if a violation of the anti-compact law had occurred. Nashville lawyer, Moreau Pinckney Estes, represented Lulu during this high profile case which made all the state newspapers. Folk heard many testimonies over several months and finally, in June of 1909, ruled that the anti-compact law had indeed been violated.

In 1913, Lulu lobbied for appointment as Clarksville's postmaster. If so appointed, she would have become the second woman in

Clarksville's history to hold that post. The post this time was denied her when, at the last moment, she was told that a woman could not hold the post.

In 1918, Lulu went into business with her father in running Clarksville's Arlington Hotel, which they renamed the Hotel Montgomery. On October 6, 1919, the hotel distinguished itself by housing the first bank in the world staffed and managed by women. The First Woman's Bank of Tennessee operated under Brenda Vineyard Runyon, founder and president, until 1926. Lulu herself was the first depositor.

Tennessee enacted legislation in April of 1919 for women to vote in Presidential and municipal elections. In preparation for an upcoming Woman Voters' Conference in Nashville and a municipal election in late May 1920, Lulu Epperson sent out a call for women to attend a May 3rd meeting at her hotel. The purpose was to help women become informed about the issues and develop a full understanding of the responsibilities of enfranchisement. Lulu served as Chair of the Woman Voters League for the Clarksville area, attended the Nashville Conference and served on some of the most important committees.

On August 18, 1920, Tennessee became the last state needed to ratify the 19th Amendment giving women the right to vote. Lulu stepped right up and organized Clarksville's first Democratic Women's Club and held its meeting at the hotel.

Clarksville celebrated its sesquicentennial in 1934. Lulu served on the hospitality committee under Mrs. Austin Peay. Lulu continued to operate the hotel until 1935. She died in Clarksville in 1964.

By Carolyn Stier Ferrell, retired teacher, author of eight Clarksville history books, member of Arts and Heritage Development Committee, Volunteer Researcher, 2020 Vision, Clarksville, TN

Emma L. Polk LaPrade

Hosted Clarksville Equal Suffrage League meetings in her home; attended Women Voters' Convention in Nashville, May 1920; Ratification Committee and charter member of Clarksville-Montgomery County League of Women Voters

Emma L. Polk was born October 10, 1856 in Robertson County, TN to Abie Long and Thomas B. Polk. She lived there until her November 19, 1901 marriage at the age of 45 to 60 year old Gustavus A. LaPrade. They resided for a short time in Birmingham, AL before settling in Clarksville by 1910.

The Clarksville Equal Suffrage League met in the LaPrades' Madison Street home multiple times. At the September 17, 1914 meeting, one of the speakers was Mrs. Lockhart H. Wallis, President of the Woman's Political Union of Houston, TX.

In 1920, Emma LaPrade was one of the Clarksville women who attended the May 18th Women Voters' Convention in Nashville. Billed as the last Tennessee suffrage convention, its intent was to continue to advocate for and prepare women to participate as responsible voters.

Active in the Clarksville League of Women Voters, Emma LaPrade was a member of the Ratification Committee and helped plan the July 26th reception held for Gov. Roberts at the Women's Club to show support and urge him on toward the ratification of the Federal Amendment.

In her later years, Emma moved into the Bellview Apartments, very modern and the first of their kind in Clarksville. She lived there until in declining health she went to stay with her sister Blanch Polk Smith in Adairville, KY where she died June 12, 1932 at age 76.

By Brenda Harper, volunteer researcher, 2020 Vision Committee, Clarksville, TN

Emma Higgins Lupton

Speaker, host, Vice-President and Publicity Chair for Clarksville Equal Suffrage League; Chair of League of Women Voters for 6th Congressional District; organizer, Vice-President, Ratification Committee and charter member of Clarksville-Montgomery County League of Women Voters

Emma Jane Higgins was born April 28, 1874 in Athens, AL to Molly Sartain and Hiram A. Higgins. Emma and her sister Clara were still quite young when their father died in the Memphis yellow fever epidemic of 1876. Emma married Henry McCluskey Lupton November 18, 1895 in Davidson County, TN. The couple was living in Clarksville when their only child Henry, Jr. was born December 16, 1896. By 1900 they were well-established, Henry working as a bookkeeper in a tobacco business, Emma as a church organist, and owning their home at 518 Commerce Street.

Emma Lupton was one of the organizers of the Clarksville Equal Suffrage League's July 31, 1914 meeting. She was the Vice-President and gave one of the primary speeches at the event. She remained consistently active in the organization. She was Publicity Chair in 1917 and hosted a meeting in her home February 28, 1918.

Tennessee enacted legislation in April of 1919 for women to vote in Presidential and municipal elections. Announcements from election officials took note that local women were slow to register: "It would seem that the ladies are not taking very enthusiastically to their new privilege, as it is estimated that less than 100 had registered up to this morning." Emma was quick to respond with her commentary in the newspaper: "The suffragists of Clarksville expect to register and do their part, even excusing Brother Osborn's comment that they all did not rush down madly the first two hot days and clamor for a registration blank..."

In April of 1920 as Chair of the League of Women Voters for 6th Congressional District, Emma Lupton put out a call to all the women's clubs in the district to participate in the May 18-19 convention in

Nashville to prepare themselves for the new responsibilities of citizenship. She also promulgated the League's endorsement of the Governor's call for the legislature to address the issue of establishing a poll tax for women in the interest of equality. At the May 3, 1920 meeting of the Clarksville women, Emma Lupton was endorsed as a member of the State Democratic Committee. Emma was among the group of Clarksville women who attended the Nashville convention.

In preparation for the May 29, 1920 municipal school bond election, two mass meetings were held to inform women about registration, voting and the school bond issue. Emma Lupton opened the May 7th meeting and introduced the speakers.

In July 1920 Emma Lupton presided over the organizing meeting and election of officers for the Clarksville-Montgomery County League of Women Voters. The focus of the league was to be the ratification of the proposed federal amendment with the 25 charter members committed to the task. She was Vice-President, on the Ratification Committee and a charter member of the league. She helped plan, issued the invitations and introduced the Governor at the reception held for him by the League when he visited Clarksville on July 26, 1920. All of which was successfully intended to show support and urge him on toward the ratification of the Federal Amendment.

Emma Lupton had additional involvements in the community throughout her life. She was a music teacher for many years, the organist at Madison Street Methodist Church and a member of the Monday Evening Music Club. She was a Charter member of the Montgomery County Historical Society in the 1920's. In 1942 she wrote an extensive history of the Madison Street Methodist Church. She died April 9, 1955 at 80 years of age.

By Brenda Harper, volunteer researcher, 2020 Vision Committee, Clarksville, TN

Stella Thayer Morgan

President of the Clarksville Equal Suffrage League in 1914 and speaker at multiple meetings; 3rd Chair of CESL in 1917; attended Woman Voters' Convention in Nashville, May 1920

Stella Rocelia Thayer was born September 29, 1879 to Emma Markham and Orris E. Thayer in Frewsburg, New York. She was working as a public school teacher and residing with her parents in Brooklyn, Kings County, NY in 1905. In the same county the following year, she married Alfred Cookman Morgan on December 6th. They had relocated to Clarksville by 1910 where he was employed as an entomologist with the U. S. Department of Agriculture.

Stella Morgan was the President of the Clarksville Equal Suffrage League in 1914. She spoke at the July 31st meeting and again when the CESL met on September 17th. She was 3rd Chair of the League in 1917 and attended the May 1920 Women Voters' Convention in Nashville. Billed as the last Tennessee suffrage convention, its intent was to continue to advocate for and prepare women to participate as responsible voters.

Stella Morgan left Tennessee to live in Tacoma, Washington sometime after 1943. She died there November 19, 1961, but her remains were returned to Clarksville for burial in Greenwood Cemetery.

By Brenda Harper, volunteer researcher, 2020 Vision Committee, Clarksville, TN

Olivia Blackman Pickering

Secretary, Clarksville Equal Suffrage League; Ratification Committee and Charter Member, Clarksville-Montgomery County League of Women Voters

Olivia Blackman was born in Clarksville, TN on November 6, 1860 to Mary Elizabeth Byrne and Oliver M. Blackman. The Blackman household as recorded in the 1870 Federal Census included a young man with no known relationship to the family, but with a unique place in the history of woman suffrage in Tennessee. Guy W. Wines as representative from Montgomery County to the 35th Session of the State General Assembly (1867-69) proposed the first legislation to grant suffrage to women in Tennessee.

Olivia had lost her mother by 1880 and was keeping house for her father and siblings. She married Lee Ely Pickering October 19, 1882. They had two children, Alice in 1883 and Oliver in 1886. Olivia Pickering lived in Clarksville, TN until her death October 4, 1940 at age 79.

Olivia Pickering was Secretary of the Clarksville Equal Suffrage League in 1917. In May of 1920 she attended the Woman Voters' Convention in Nashville. Billed as the last annual Tennessee suffrage convention, its intent was to continue to advocate for and prepare women to participate as responsible voters.

Olivia Pickering was active in the Clarksville League of Women Voters, a member of the Ratification Committee and helped plan the reception held for Gov. Roberts at the Women's Club to show support and urge him on toward the ratification of the Federal Amendment.

By Brenda Harper, volunteer researcher, 2020 Vision Committee, Clarksville, TN

Lou Redd Roach

Chair of the Clarksville Equal Suffrage League in 1917, attended Woman Voters' Convention in Nashville, May 1920; Ratification Committee and charter member of Clarksville-Montgomery County League of Women Voters

Lou Redd Roach was born in Trigg County, KY on June 6, 1866 to Mary Thompson and Stapleton Redd. She spent most of her girlhood in Hopkinsville, KY where she attended South Kentucky College. She married Robert Cook Roach February 8, 1887 and had five daughters. They had moved to Clarksville by 1888 where she resided until her death August 18, 1937.

In 1917 Lou Roach was the Chair of the Clarksville Equal Suffrage League. In 1920 she was one of the Clarksville women who attended the May 18th Women Voters' Convention in Nashville. Billed as the last Tennessee suffrage convention, its intent was to continue to advocate for and prepare women to participate as responsible voters.

She was active in the Clarksville League of Women Voters, a member of the Ratification Committee and helped plan the July 26th reception held for Gov. Roberts at the Women's Club to show support and urge him on toward the ratification of the Federal Amendment.

By Brenda Harper, volunteer researcher, 2020 Vision Committee, Clarksville, TN

Source documentation of research findings is posted with the biographies:

Online Biographical Dictionary of the Woman Suffrage Movement in the United States
https://documents.alexanderstreet.com/VOTESforWOMEN

Recipes from
Clarksville's Suffragists

Fannie Miller Hodgson and Lee Hodgson

The recipes in this section were contributed by our Suffragists to the cook books listed below. They have been included here as written with minor clarifications or corrections of obvious errors.

Southern Delight, Compiled by The Art Study Class and the Dilettanti, Titus Printers, Clarksville, TN, 1923

Dixie Dishes, Compiled by The Art Study Class and The Ringgold Home Demonstration Club, printed by Titus, Clarksville, TN, 1924

The Green Book: Dixie Dishes, Compiled by the Federation of Women's Clubs, Titus Printing Co., Clarksville, TN, 1930

The C.F.W.C. Gold Cook Book, Clarksville Federation of Women's Clubs, no publication data, no date

My Old Clarksville Cook Book, no publication data, no date

Thank you

Melissa Miller, Customs House Museum Collection

Francis Ross

Barbara Wilbur

for sharing your historic cook books.

Emma Higgins Lupton

Banbury Tarts

2 cups seeded raisins	Grated rind and juice of 2 lemons
2 eggs, beaten	2 cups sugar
1 tablespoon sherry	8 tart shells

Run raisins through food chopper, add other ingredients, mix well and fill tart shells. Bake in hot oven at 400 for 20 minutes.

Mrs. Henry Lupton   *The CFWC Cook Book*

Ice-box Pudding

¼ pound powdered sugar	¼ pound butter
4 eggs	¼ pound Mallard's chocolate
¼ pound shredded almonds	¼ pound macaroons
2 teaspoonfuls vanilla	1 teaspoonful vinegar
Whipped cream	

Cream yolks with sugar, butter and melted chocolate, Pour vinegar over macaroons. Beat egg white to a still froth. Mix all ingredients and place in ice-box twelve hours. Slice and serve with whipped cream.

Mrs. Henry Lupton   *Southern Delight* 1923

Chocolate Caramels

1 cupful granulated sugar
1 cupful brown sugar
2 cupfuls milk
1 cupful corn syrup
2 squares chocolate
1 teaspoon vanilla

Boil sugar, milk and syrup. When nearly done, add grated or shaved chocolate. Cook until mixture forms a hard ball in water. Beat until stiff enough to spread and when cool enough to cut in squares. If canned milk is used, add ¼ teaspoonful soda.

Mrs. Henry Lupton   *Dixie Dishes* 1924

Brenda Vineyard Runyon

Transparent Pies
9 eggs, save aside 6 whites
1 wineglass or ¼ cup wine
1 lb sugar, sifted
2 nutmegs, grated
½ lb butter
(Makes about 3 nine-inch pies or 18 small tarts)
Cream butter and sugar, add eggs (3 whole eggs plus 6 yolks) and beat until sponge-light. Add wine and nutmeg. Pour into unbaked pie shells and put into 450 oven for 5 minutes. Reduce heat to 375 and bake until firm, 20-25 minutes. Test firmness by shaking pan slightly.
Meringue: 6 egg whites   dash of salt
              3 rounded Tbsp sugar   1½ tsp vanilla
Beat 6 egg whites with a dash of salt until stiff. Add sugar and vanilla. Meringue should stand in peaks. Spoon over cooled pies (or meringue will "weep") and run under broiler until golden brown.
Mrs. Frank J. Runyon   The CFWC Gold Cook Book

Annie Mimms Prince Winn

Sponge Jelly Roll
3 eggs, yolks and whites beaten separately
1 cupful sugar
1 cupful flour
2 tablespoonfuls water
Pinch salt
1 teaspoonful baking powder
Add sugar to the well-beaten yolks, then water, salt, flour, baking powder and last fold in the beaten whites. Bake in well-greased shallow pan. Turn out on damp towel. Spread jelly, then roll.
Mrs. Annie M. Winn   *Dixie Dishes* 1924

Mary Hunt Marks Gholson

Chicken Salad
Boil a fat hen slowly until thoroughly done. Add 3 slices of bacon and 1 onion half an hour before taking from fire. Let cool in stock. If fancy dish is desires, use the white meat only, otherwise the whole hen. Cut meat and half as much celery in cubes. Mix with either French dressing or mayonnaise and dot with capers.
Mrs. A. R. Gholson   *The CFWC Gold Cook Book*

Fancy Chocolate Pudding with Cake
Make a large opening in the center of a yellow sponge cake. Place cake on a large platter. Pour sauce over cake while still hot. Heap whipped cream in center.
Sauce: Boil ½ cup sugar with 1½ cups water to make syrup. Blend 6 Tbsp shaved chocolate or 1/3 cup cocoa with 2 Tbsp flour and a little water. Add syrup to this mixture with a pinch of salt. Boil a few minutes. Remove from heat and add ½ tsp vanilla.
Mrs. A. R. Gholson   *The CFWC Gold Cook Book*

Oatmeal Macaroons

2 eggs	½ cup sugar
1 Tbsp melted butter	¼ tsp salt
1 tsp vanilla	2½ cups rolled oats

Beat eggs light and whip in the sugar. Add other ingredients in order given. Mix thoroughly. Drop from a teaspoon onto a well-oiled cookie sheet, shaping into symmetrical rounds. Bake in moderate oven.
Mary Hunt Marks Gholson   Provided from her recipe stash by great granddaughter, Julia Marks Meadows. Submitted by Rubye Patch.

Orange Marmalade
Strain the juice of 12 lemons and grind 12 large oranges. Measure juice and pulp. Add an equal quantity of cold water and of sugar. Let stand 24 hours, then boil until thick. Seal in glass jars.
Mrs. A. R. Gholson   *The Green Cook Book: Dixie Dishes* 1930

White Icing

3 egg whites	3 cupfuls granulated sugar
1 cupful boiling water	2 teaspoonfuls baking powder
1 teaspoonful cream of tartar	1 teaspoonful vanilla

Boil water, sugar, cream of tartar and baking powder without stirring.
Test by stirring a little of the syrup in a saucer. When it begins to turn
white, pour slowly into the well-beaten egg whites then add vanilla.
Set bowl in pan of cold water; beat until cold. If icing is too hard, add
a little water. If soft, cover and let stand several hours if necessary.
Mrs. A. R. Gholson   *The Green Cook Book: Dixie Dishes* 1930

Fannie Miller Hodgson

Meat Pie

Pastry:	Filling:
I pint flour	3 pints cold meat, ground
2 teaspoons lard	1 quart stock
1 teaspoon salt	2 tablespoonfuls butter
1 teaspoonful sugar	1 onion, minced
2 teaspoonfuls yeast powder	1 carrot, minced
1 gill water, cold [gill = 4 ounces]	3 tablespoonfuls flour
Salt and pepper	

Mrs. Lee Hodgson   *Dixie Dishes* 1924

Charlotte Russe

½ box gelatin dissolved in ¼ cup cold water
1 cup sweet milk
2 egg yolks
1 quart whipping cream
Bring milk to a boil with gelatin added. Beat yolks adding 2 teaspoons
of sugar. Add them to milk and cook until thick. When done, add to
whipped cream and beat until gelatin is set. Add 3 teaspoons sugar
and 1 teaspoon vanilla. Pour into a dish lined with lady fingers.
Mrs. Lee M. Hodgson   *My Old Clarksville Cook Book*

Bennie Gill Fort

Brown Bread

7 cups graham flour	2 cups dark molasses
2 cups corn meal	1 cup sugar
4 cups buttermilk	4 tsp soda

Mix all ingredients well and fill 1 lb. baking powder cans half full. Steam 3 hours and dry in moderate oven 2 or 3 minutes.

Mrs. Dancey Fort   *CFWC Cook Book*

Puff Paste

1 rounded cupful sifted pastry	¼ teaspoon salt
¾ cupful butter	about ¼ cupful cold water

Method: Mix flour and salt, cut in butter with two knives hours before until resembles coarse meal, then remove about 2/3 of it. To the first third add cold water a little at a time to make a stiff smooth dough. Roll out again and repeat process with remaining butter. Fold paste several times and chill 1 or 2 hours before using. Unfold, roll out 1/3 inch thick, fit loosely into the pan and cut off about ¼ inch beyond rim. Fit and push edge onto rim in scallops. (When a top crust with dry crumbs or flour, or brush with egg before filling to prevent sogginess. Paste shells for patties, tarts, etc. are easily made by inverting individual fluted pans and fitting paste on the outside. Prick well and bake until slightly browned.

Plain Paste

Level measure:

1½ cupfuls pastry flour	1 teaspoonful salt
½ cupful Crisco	4 to 6 tablespoons cold water

Mix flour and salt, cut in shortening until like coarse meal, add just enough water to make a stiff paste, roll out lightly, fit in pans and proceed as in Puff Paste. Place in a hot oven and bake for ten minutes and then reduce heat.

Mrs. Dancey Fort   *Dixie Dishes* 1924

Lois Towsend Cunningham

Country Boiled Ham

Soak overnight in cold water, one fifteen pound Hampshire ham; wash thoroughly and place in covered boiler of boiling water, adding boiling as it boils away. Cook until skin begins to wrinkle; remove and place on a platter to cool. Remove skins and loosened bones and when cold, dress one inch all over with grated crumbs, black pepper and brown sugar. Brown in moderate oven. Never slice until perfectly cold.

Lois T. Cunningham   *Southern Delight* 1923

Fruit Salad

Dice six firm ripe bananas, 1 fresh pineapple or I can sliced pineapple, 4 oranges and 1 grapefruit. Sprinkle lightly with powdered sugar and place in colander on platter on ice for at least two hours. Dress lightly, serve on lettuce hearts and garnish with whipped cream and red or green cherries.

Fruit Salad Dressing:

Whip well yolks of 4 eggs, add juice of 4 large lemons, 2 tablespoons sugar and ¼ teaspoon nutmeg liquid flavoring. Cook in a double-boiler until very thick. When cold add 1 cupful stiff whipped cream. Pecans or almonds may be added if well crisped.

Lois T. Cunningham   *Southern Delight* 1923

Lulu Bringhurst Epperson

Sally Lunn

1 pint flour	2 teaspoonfuls baking powder
1¼ cupfuls milk	Butter size of an egg
2 tablespoons sugar	

Mix as you would a cake. Cook in hot well-oiled moulds or pans.

Mrs. Lulu B. Epperson *Dixie Dishes* 1924

Mildred Crouch Savage Catlett

Pineapple Frappe

3 cups sugar

1 cup water

3 egg whites, beaten

1 can grated pineapple

Milk and cream

Boil sugar and water until it strings from the spoon. Pour this syrup over the beaten whites of three eggs and beat to a smooth cream. To this add a can of grates pineapple and as much cream and milk as will make the quantity you require. Let it get cold and freeze.

Mrs. Howard Savage   *The Green Book: Dixie Dishes* 1930

Round Steak en Casserole

2 pounds round steak cut 1 inch or more in thickness

1 cupful flour

1 onion, chopped fine

Salt and Pepper

Place steak on meat board, trim and season with salt and pepper. Sprinkle part of the flour over one side of the steak and pound thoroughly with a meat ponder. Turn over and repeat this operation on the other side. Cut into individual pieces. Cover bottom of casserole with hot water, add meat and onion, cover with more water. Closely cover dish and bake from two to three hours. Add water occasionally if necessary. Send to the table in the casserole or on hot platter garnished with squares of toast and parsley.

Mrs. Howard Savage   *Dixie Dishes* 1924

Corn Pudding

Prepared pulp from 6 ears or 1 can of corn

1 Tbsp butter

1 tsp sugar

½ cup milk

Salt and pepper

Mix all ingredients well, pour into buttered dish and sprinkle with flour. Bake 30 to 40 minutes (if using fresh corn) in 350 oven. For canned corn, 20 minutes. Serves 4.

Mrs. Richard Catlett   The CWFC Cook Book

Katherine Hoey Boillin

Angel Custard

1 quart milk	4 egg whites, whipped
1 tablespoonful sugar	2 drops almond extract
1 teaspoonful vanilla	grated Macaroon crumbs

Heat milk in double-boiler, pour slowly on the stiffly whipped egg whites, then add sugar, almond and vanilla extract. Turn into custard cups. Set the cups in a pan of hot water and cook in a moderate oven until firm, then cover the tops with grated macaroon crumbs.

Mrs. Joseph A. Boillin   *Dixie Dishes* 1924

Toasted English Muffins

½ cake compressed yeast	2¼ cupfuls warm milk
3 tablespoonfuls melted butter	1 quart flour
1 teaspoonful salt	1 teaspoonful sugar

Dissolve yeast in ¼ cupful milk. Then add with rest of milk to the dry ingredients. Beat mixture well. Add the beaten egg and melted butter. Beat well for about ten minutes. Cover, set in a warm place to rise. Have well-greased muffin rings ready. When mixture is light, half fill each ring and bake. When done, slice in two and toast. Serve with butter and syrup.

Mrs. Joseph A. Boillin   *Southern Delight* 1923

Apple Fritters

1 cupful sifted pastry flour	¼ teaspoon salt
1 level teaspoon baking powder	1 teaspoon sugar
1 egg, beaten lightly	¼ cupful milk
2 apples, pared and cut in small pieces	hot fat for frying

Sift together, three times, the flour, salt, baking powder and sugar. Add the milk to the beaten egg and stir in the dry ingredients. The stir in the bits of apple. Drop the batter into the fat by spoonfuls and let fry until delicately browned. Drain on soft paper. Serve with powdered sugar or jelly sauce. Can use any other fruit the same way.

Mrs. Joseph A. Boillin   *Southern Delight* 1923

Ethel Collier Dickson

Delicious Chicken Ring or Loaf

4 or 5 cups cooked, chopped chicken	1 cup cooked rice
1 small can pimientos, chopped	1 cup bread crumbs
3 eggs, beaten	¼ lb butter

Melt butter and mix with other ingredients. Season to taste. Pack into greased ring mold or loaf pan and bake 45 minutes at 350. Meanwhile, make the following sauce:

3 Tbsp flour	1 cup canned mushrooms and liquid
3 Tbsp butter	2 cups milk

Stir flour into melted butter and cook until smooth. Add milk and mushroom liquid, cooking and stirring constantly until smooth and thick. Add mushrooms and season to taste. Keep sauce hot in a double boiler until ready to serve. Unmold chicken mixture on hot platter and cover with sauce. Garnish with paprika and sprigs of parsley.

Mrs. J. Moore Dickson   *The CWFC Gold Cook Book*

Apricot Ice

Drain and strain a 2 pond can of apricots. Add juice to pulp and mix with 1 cupful of sugar, ¼ cupful lemon juice, ¼ cupful grape juice. Freeze partly and fold in a pint of whipped cream.

Mrs. J. Moore Dickson   *Dixie Dishes* 1924

Apple Casserole

Peel and slice 8 apples, tart preferred
1½ cups sugar
Juice of 1 lemon and 1 orange
Combine all and cook covered until apples are tender. Remove cover and continue cooking slowly until juice is gone. Pour into a buttered casserole, dot with butter and bake 15 to 20 minutes at 350 or moderate heat.

Mrs. J. Moore Dickson   *The CFWC Gold Cook Book*

Grandmother's Pound Cake
Grease tube cake pan, flour lightly.
Sift 2 cupfuls pastry flour (measure after sifting), sift again 5 times and set aside. Break 5 whole eggs into 1 generous cupful fresh butter. When well-creamed (use hand to mix this cake), add 1 2/3 cupfuls of sugar sifted a little at a time. Work until sugar loses its grain and beat until no egg can be seen. Beat hard and long, the longer the better. Add flour, beat again and when it is a creamy mass, flavor with 1 tablespoonful rose water and 1 teaspoonful vanilla if desired. Put by handfuls into the pan, shake down and bake in a slow oven. Time for baking about 50 minutes. Ice or not.
Mrs. J. Moore Dickson   *Dixie Dishes* 1924

Olivia Blackman Pickering

Beaten Biscuit

1 quart flour	1 tsp sugar
1 tsp salt	¾ cup lard or substitute
1 tsp baking soda	1 cup milk

Sift dry ingredients together, add lard, mix well then add milk.
Mix all thoroughly, roll out or beat till dough blisters, use small cutter and bake in moderate oven.
Mrs. Lee Pickering   *The CFWC Gold Cook Book*

Chile Sauce

24 large ripe tomatoes	4 white onions
3 green peppers	3 Tbsp. salt
1 Tbsp cinnamon	1½ Tbsp. ground cloves & allspice
1 cupful sugar	3 cupfuls vinegar

Chop tomatoes, onions, peppers. Add remaining ingredients. Boil slowly three hours. Bottle and seal.
Mrs. Lee Pickering   *Southern Delight* 1923

Wilhelmina Sickenberger Barksdale

Olympia Pan Roast
Put into a stew kettle, one quart very small oysters, I cup catsup, 1½ tsp Worcestershire sauce, a large lump of butter and salt to taste. Let mixture come to a boil. Have hot slices of buttered toast ready. Pour pan roast over toast and serve at once. Should serve 6.
Mrs. W. W. Barksdale   *The CWFC Gold Cook Book*

Superb Meat Loaf

2 lbs round steak	1 minced onion
½ lb fresh pork	1 Tbsp salt
2 cups bread crumbs	½ tsp baking powder
2 cups milk	¼ tsp pepper
1 egg, beaten	1 Tbsp minced parsley
1 can tomato soup	1 cup boiling water

Have ground or grind meat twice. Soak crumbs in milk. Mix all ingredients except soup and water. Mold into loaf, put in a greased pan and sear in 450 oven for 10 minutes. Pour soup and water over loaf. Reduce heat to 350 and bake I hour, basting often. Serve sliced with gravy. Serves 12 or more.
Mrs. W. W. Barksdale, Sr.   *The CWFC Gold Cook Book*

Pearl Darnell Perkins

Potatoes Baked with Cheese
Six large baked or boiled potatoes in jackets
One-third cupful hot milk
Two teaspoonfuls salt
One-fourth pound shredded yellow cheese
One-eighth teaspoonful paprika
Cut potatoes in half lengthwise and scoop out centers. Heat milk, add cheese and cook until smooth. Mix with potatoes, add seasoning and beat until light. Refill potato shells and bake in hot oven ten minutes.
Mrs. Frank Perkins   *The Green Book: Dixie Dishes* 1930

Emma Polk LaPrade

Fresh Fruit Cocktail

6 oranges	1 ½ cups sugar
3 grapefruits	1 small bottle maraschino cherries
1 small can pineapple	

Peel and cut citrus fruits in small pieces, add pineapple, sugar and chopped cherries. Mix well and refrigerate for several hours before serving. Attractive served in cups made from the orange skins for smaller servings; from the grapefruits for larger servings.

Mrs. G. A. LaPrade   *The CFWC Gold Cook Book*

Oyster Pie

1 quart oysters	Pastry shell, crumbs or flour
4-6 hard-boiled eggs	2 medium cooked sliced potatoes

Make rich pastry to line and cover deep pie pan. Sprinkle pastry with crumbs or flour. Put in layer of drained oysters, one of eggs sliced, top with potatoes and sprinkle with salt, pepper and dot with butter. Repeat layers and cover with pastry. Bake 30 minutes at 400 or until nicely browned. Serves 6.

Mrs. G. A. LaPrade   *The CFWC Gold Cook Book*

Dressing or Stuffing

Mix equal quantities of corn meal, egg bread and stale white bread. Add chopped onion, parsley and celery. Salt and pepper to taste. Moisten with melted butter or drippings and stock.

Mrs. G. A. LaPrade   *The CFWC Gold Cook Book*

Peach Preserves

Peel peaches, quarter and weigh. Match with an equal amount of sugar and just enough water to make a thick syrup. Turn peaches into hot syrup, cooking until transparent. Remove peaches and cook syrup until very thick. Put peaches back in syrup, boil 2 minutes and seal in glass jars.

Mrs. G. A. LaPrade   *The CFWC Gold Cook Book*

Ethel Wilder Bailey

All-in-One Supper Casserole

1½ lbs ground beef or pork	2 Irish potatoes, peeled & diced
1 medium can peas	2 carrots, peeled and diced
Several slices onion	salt and pepper

1 can tomato soup or 1 medium bottle tomato catsup

Make meat balls from ground meat, seasoning to taste. Put vegetables in greased casserole in layers. Top with meat balls and cover with catsup or soup. Bake in a 350 oven for 2½ or 3 hours.

Mrs. C. W. Bailey   *The CWFC Gold Cook Book*

Scrambled Bacon and Corn

(Quick dish for breakfast or supper)

8 slices diced bacon	¼ cup milk
½ can creamed corn	¼ tsp salt
2 eggs, beaten light	¼ tsp pepper

Cook bacon in deep skillet until slightly brown; add corn, stirring until hot through. Add eggs to which milk and seasoning have been added and stir until eggs are set. Serve on hot buttered toast. Have everything at hand as eggs cook quickly.

Mrs. C. W. Bailey   *The CWFC Gold Cook Book*

Fresh Fruit Pies

Make a large pastry shell (or several individual ones) as usual, over an inverted pie pan, pricking it well before baking so it will keep its shape. Just before serving, fill it with sweetened sliced fruit or berries and top with whipped cream.

Mrs. C. W. Bailey   *My Old Clarksville Cook Book*

Willie Erwin Daniel

Silver Lake Chocolate Cream Pie

1¼ cups sifted Swans Down Cake Flour	¼ tsp baking powder
1 cup sugar	2 eggs, well-beaten
3 Tbsp butter or other shortening	½ cup milk

Sift flour once, measure, add baking powder and sift together 3 times. Cream butter thoroughly, add ½ cup sugar gradually and cream together until light and fluffy. Add remaining sugar to eggs and beat well. Add flour, alternately with milk, a small amount at a time. Beat after each addition until smooth. Bake in 2 greased 8-inch layer pans in moderate oven for 20 minutes.

Cool. Split each layer in half. Put together and cover top with chocolate frosting and filling. Double the receipt for 3 9-inch layers.

Chocolate Frosting and Filling:
4 squares Baker's unsweetened chocolate, cut in pieces

1½ cups sugar	1 Tbsp butter
½ cup cold milk	1 tsp vanilla
2 egg yolks, well-beaten	

Add chocolate to milk and place over low flame. Cook until mixture is smooth and blended, stirring constantly. Beat egg yolks with 3 Tbsp sugar. Add remaining sugar to chocolate mixture and cook until smooth. Add egg mixture and butter and cook 1 minute. Remove from fire. Add vanilla. Beat until thick and creamy. Spread between layers and on top of Silver Lake House Chocolate Cream Pie.

Willie E. Daniel   *The CWFC Gold Cook Book*

Chicken Creole

2 cups chopped cooked chicken	½ cup broken pecans
1 cups rich white sauce	grated nutmeg
Worchestershire sauce	Tabasco sauce

Mix chicken, white sauce and nuts. Flavor highly with sauces and nutmeg. Serve very hot in timbales or on buttered toast.

Mrs, W. M. Daniel, Sr.   *The CWFC Gold Cook Book*

Chicken Pie

Pastry: 1 cup flour
            2 rounded Tbsp lard
            3 Tbsp water

Work lard into sifted flour, add water and mix quickly, handling as little as possible. Refrigerate 2 hours then line baking dish, saving enough dough for top. Bake in hot oven at 450 for 12 to 15 minutes or until light brown.

Filling: 1 chicken cooked, chopped   1 can mushrooms
          1 pint cooked potatoes, cubed   1 tsp minced parsley
          Enough white sauce & chicken stock mixed well to fill dish

Put on top crust and bake to a golden brown in 350 oven for 25-30 minutes, Serves 6 to 8.

Mrs. W. M. Daniel, Sr.   *The CWFC Gold Cook Book*

Grace Pratt Stacker

Charlotte Russe

1 pkg gelatin   1 cup sugar
¼ cup cold milk   2 eggs, beaten separately
½ pint whipping cream   1 tsp vanilla
½ cup milk   Lady Fingers

Soften gelatin in ¼ cup cold milk.

Beat sugar and egg yolks well and add the remaining ½ cup milk. Cook this in a double boiler until mixture begins to thicken. Stir in gelatin. Remove from heat and cool.

Fold custard into whipped cream a little at a time. Then fold stiffly beaten egg whites in carefully and add vanilla.

Line bowl with Lady Fingers. Pour in mixture and chill until firm.

Mrs. Clay Stacker   *The CWFC Gold Cook Book*

Maria Stacker Ellis

Baking Powder Biscuit

1 pint flour	1 teaspoonful salt
2 teaspoonfuls baking powder	2 tablespoonfuls fat

1/3 cupful milk or water (more or less)

Mix dry ingredients and sift; cut in fat with knife and fork. Make hole in center of mixture; pour in liquid; mix lightly with spoon; making dough as soft as can be handled. Toss lightly on floured board; roll to ½ inch thickness. Cut into rounds and cook 10 minutes in a hot oven or at 415 F.

Maria Stacker Ellis   *Dixie Dishes* 1924

Hot Tamale Roll

1 ½ pounds meat (chicken or round steak)	2 cans tomato sauce
½ teaspoonfuls chili powder or more	Garlic

1 pod of red pepper & enough ground red pepper to make it hot

1 pint of corn meal	1 onion
1 tablespoonful lard	1 ½ teaspoonfuls salt

Boil meat till it falls in pieces, grind fine then add seasonings, tomato sauce, chili, onion and garlic. Scald the meal with the meat stock, add salt and lard, make stiff mush and spread on a piece of wet cheese cloth 12 by 20 inches. Cover this with a layer of the meat mixture using the cloth to keep it in shape. Tie up in the cloth and boil it in the meat stock. Corn shucks may be used instead of cloth if procurable.

Maria S. Ellis   *Dixie Dishes* 1924

Spiced Tea

½ - 1 teaspoonful tea	1 cupful boiling water

Add tea to boiling water, remove from fire, steep five minutes. Add water in which whole cloves and whole allspice have been boiled for an hour or more. The quantity must be decided by individual taste. One teaspoonful of spice should flavor four or five cupfuls of tea. Sweeten and add orange juice to taste.

Maria S. Ellis   *Dixie Dishes* 1924

Sallie Hurst Peay

Bavarian Cream
1 quart sweet cream or 1 pint each light cream and whipping cream
2 pkgs gelatin
½ cup cold water
4 egg yolks
1 cup sugar
2 tsp vanilla
Soften gelatin in water. Scald light cream and pour over egg yolks and sugar which have been beaten together until light and fluffy. Heat in double boiler, stirring constantly until mixture begins to thicken. Remove from heat, add gelatin and stir until dissolved and cool. Add vanilla, fold in whipped cream and pour into mold. Chill until firm.
Mrs. Austin Peay   *The CFWC Gold Cook Book*

Enola Rudolph

Steamed Icing

6 egg whites   3 cupfuls sugar
1 cupful water   1 teaspoonful lemon juice
1 teaspoonful vanilla

When whites are pretty well beaten, add ½ cupful sugar. Boil water and remaining sugar about five minutes. Add a little of this syrup to beaten whites and beat, then add more syrup, which has been boiling slowly and beat again. Before adding last portion of syrup, it should form a hard ball when a little is dropped into cold water. Add 1 teaspoon lemon juice and steam over boiling water, constantly beating until think and glossy. Add I teaspoonful vanilla. Beat and beat.
Mrs. R. S. Rudolph   *Dixie Dishes* 1924

Petinka Bailey Foskett

Rhubarb Pie
2 heaping cups fresh rhubarb (cut in ½ inch pieces)
2 Tbsp flour
1 egg
1 cup sugar
1 Tbsp butter
Mix flour with sugar and butter, stir gradually into egg and beat until mixture is creamy and smooth. Pour rhubarb into unbaked pie shell and spread evenly with egg mixture. Put on top crust and bake about 45 minutes at 375.
Petinka B. Foskett   *The CFWC Gold Cook Book*

White Sauce
1/3 cupful flour
2 tablespoonfuls butter
1 cupful milk
Blend butter and flour on stove and add milk. Cook until thick.
Petinka B. Foskett   *Dixie Dishes* 1924

Chicken a la King

4 to 6 chicken breasts, cooked	2 or 3 bay leaves
Salt, pepper, paprika	2 Tbsp flour
5 Tbsp butter	1 cup cream
1 small onion, chopped fine	¼ cup wine
1 green pepper, chopped fine	1 can mushrooms

Cut chicken into fairly large pieces and season lightly with salt and pepper. Melt 3 Tbsp butter and saute chicken in it. Melt other 2 Tbsp butter in sauce pan and saute onions, green peppers and bay leaves, cooking until soft, but not brown. When smooth and bubbling, add cream and wine slowly, stirring constantly. Liquid from the mushrooms may also be added, then chicken and mushrooms. Heat thoroughly and keep hot until serving in double boiler. Serves 6 to 8.
Petinka B. Foskett   *The CFWC Gold Cook Book*

Mamie Green Patch

Pimiento Sandwich

To one can well-drained pimientos, add 8 hard-boiled eggs mashed, pinch of salt and enough salad dressing to make a smooth paste. Spread on thin slices of bread.

Mrs. Ben Patch   *Dixie Dishes* 1924

Cheese Soufflé

3 tablespoonfuls flour	3 tablespoonfuls butter
3 eggs	1 cupful milk
1 cupful grated cheeses	seasoning to taste

Make a thick white sauce by blending butter and flour in a saucepan, then add milk and stir until boiling. Cool three minutes then stir in cheese and yolks of eggs beaten until thick. Season to taste. Fold in the stiffly beaten whites of eggs and bake in a greased dish about twenty-five minutes. Serve quickly.

Mrs. Ben Patch   *The Green Book: Dixie Dishes* 1930

Mustard Pickle

2 quarts large cucumbers	1 quart green tomatoes
1 quart small cucumbers	4 large heads cauliflower
2 quarts small onions	6 green peppers

Make a strong brine (strong enough to hold up an egg) and put vegetables in brine overnight. Scald in the brine the next morning, but do not boil. Drain and cover with dressing made of

1 gallon vinegar	2 cups flour
½ lb ground mustard	3 cups white sugar

Make a paste of mustard, flour and sugar with a little vinegar. Stir in rest of vinegar and bring to a boil, stirring constantly to prevent scorching. When thick and smooth (simmer about 10 minutes), pour over hot drained vegetables. Heat thoroughly and pour into sterilized jars. You will have a delicious pickle and a pretty pickle if small onions and very small cucumbers are left whole, cauliflower broken into flowerets, and other vegetables sliced or quartered.

Mamie Green Patch   *The CFWC Gold Cook Book*

Margaret Wilkerson Crouch

Chicken Soufflé
One pint cooked chicken, finely chopped
One pint cream sauce
Four eggs
One teaspoon parsley
One teaspoon onion juice
Salt and pepper
Stir chicken and seasoning into boiling sauce. Cook two minutes; add egg yolks, well-beaten. Pour into a buttered pan and bake one half-hour. Serve with mushroom sauce.
Mrs. Jack Crouch   *The Green Book: Dixie Dishes* 1930

Fruit Dessert
Clip 4 oranges, 4 bananas and 1 can pineapple.
Put layer of clipped fruit in tea glass, then a layer of vanilla ice cream, repeating until glass is full. Then pour grape juice over it.
Mrs. Jack Crouch   *Dixie Dishes* 1924

Grape Juice
Put 6 lbs grapes and 1 pint water on stove and boil a few minutes. Put on a bag and let drip several hours or overnight. Measure 1 cup sugar to each quart juice, boil 10 minutes. Bottle and cork or seal (safer) immediately.
Mrs. Jack Crouch   *The CFWC Gold Cook Book*

Carrie Wallace Wilson

Maryland Cheese Straws
Work to a smooth paste, 3 slightly heaping tablespoonfuls grated cheese. 2 tablespoonfuls flour, a little salt, cayenne pepper and a beaten egg yolk.
Roll very thin, cut in narrow strips and bake until a light brown.
Mrs. C. G. Wilson   *Dixie Dishes* 1924

Jessie Couts Beach

Café Parfait

One-half cupful strong coffee
One-half pint sugar
Two egg yolks
One pint cream

Cook coffee, sugar and egg in double boiler until consistency of thick cream. When cold, add cream which has been whipped. Freeze three hours and serve in parfait glasses with whipped cream. Serves eight.
Mrs. W. E. Beach   *The Green Book: Dixie Dishes* 1930

Crumbled Tarley

6 eggs	1 cup chopped pecans
1 cup sugar	1 cup grated bread crumbs
1 cup chopped dates	1 quart cream

Cream yolks and sugar, add other ingredients, beat well; then add beaten egg whites. Cook in a greased pan 30 minutes at 300. When done, let cool in pan, turn out, crumble and mix with 1 pint cream, whipped. The remaining pint is whipped and served with the cake. This will serve 8 people.
Mrs. W. E. Beach   *The CFWC Gold Cook Book*

Corn Fritters

1 cup drained can corn	4 Tbsp sugar
1 cup flour	3 tsp baking powder
2 eggs, slightly beaten	¼ tsp salt

Sift dry ingredients into bowl, add corn and eggs and mix just until blended. Drop from spoon into hot lard to which has been added 1 tsp vinegar. Drain fritters on paper towels and keep hot or serve immediately. If you want them sweeter, shake lightly in bag of powdered sugar or sprinkle with sugar.
Mrs. W. E. Beach   *The CFWC Gold Cook Book*

Lula Poindexter Anderson

Pressed Chicken

I large (4 lb) chicken	1 quart chicken broth
8 hard-boiled eggs	2 pkgs gelatin
1 cup chopped celery	juice of 2 lemons
Salt	pepper

Cook chicken until tender and reserve or cook down broth to 1 quart. Dice chicken and 3 or 4 of the eggs. Dissolve gelatin, soaking in ½ cup cold water and adding to hot broth. Add other ingredients and mix well. Pack half of mixture into oblong pan (about the size of a loaf pan.) Down the center of this, place whole hard-boiled eggs end to end. Carefully fill in remainder of chicken mixture and congeal. Slices look very attractive with egg centers. Serve with mayonnaise or sour cream dressing and relishes. Garnish with lettuce, parsley and lemon slices.

Mrs. W. B. Anderson   *The CFWC Gold Cook Book*

Pretty Potatoes

Select medium size Irish potatoes, peel, wipe dry and rub with lard. Bake at 400 for 40 to 60 minutes. When potatoes are half done, remove from oven, stick thickly – porcupine style – with blanched almonds and finish baking.

Mrs. W. B. Anderson   *The CFWC Gold Cook Book*

Ham and Baked Eggs

Butter a shallow baking dish and line with a thin layer of ground ham seasoned with minced parsley and celery seed. Separate as many eggs as needed being careful not to break yolks. Beat egg whites stiff and spread on ham, making a nest of whites for each yolk. Slip yolks into place, season with salt and pepper and sprinkle with grated cheese. Bake at 325 about 20 minutes or until eggs are set.

Mrs. W. B. Anderson   *The CFWC Gold Cook Book*

Stella Thayer Morgan

Topping for Chicken, Meat or Oyster Pie

5 tsp melted butter	2 cups flour
1 egg beaten slightly	3 tsp baking powder
1 cup milk	1 tsp salt

Mix ingredients lightly and pour over chicken, etc. Meat or product used must have plenty of liquid with it. Bake in 400 oven until topping is crusty and brown.

Mrs. A. C. Morgan   *The CFWC Gold Cook Book*

Pop-Corn Balls

Melt 3 teaspoons butter, add 2 cupfuls molasses and 2/3 cupful sugar. Stir until sugar is dissolved. Boil until mixture is brittle in cold water. Pour over 6 quarts freshly popped corn. Butter the tips of the fingers and shape mixture into balls.

Mrs. A. C. Morgan   *Dixie Dishes* 1924

Katherin Ireys Diehl

Ice-Tea Ginger Ale

Brew 3 or 4 teaspoonfuls tea, drop in clove. When cool, dilute, sweeten, and add juice of 1 lemon and 1 orange. When cold and ready to serve, add 2 bottles ginger ale. This will serve about eight persons.

Mrs. Charles Diehl   *Dixie Dishes* 1924

Cream Meringue

Whip whites of 7 eggs to a stiff froth and beat in gradually 1½ cupfuls sugar, add 1 teaspoonful vanilla, 1 cupful chopped nuts, then fold in ¾ cupful sugar. Put kisses, any size desired, in baking sheets covered with manila paper. Bake from 40 to 60 minutes in a very slow oven. Served with whipped cream.

Mrs. Charles Diehl   *Dixie Dishes* 1924

Frances Pollard Rudolph

Pudding a la Rudolph

6 tablespoonfuls sugar	4 tablespoonfuls butter
2 eggs	1 pint buttermilk
2 tsp soda in 1 cupful flour	2 cupfuls bread crumbs
2 teaspoonfuls salt	

3 cups chopped raisins mixed with flour
Steam three hours and serve with hard sauce.
Frances Pollard Rudolph   *Southern Delight* 1923

Coffee Bavarian

½ box gelatin	1 pint strong coffee
1 pint milk	1 cupful and 1 tsp sugar
2 eggs, separated	pinch of salt
1 pint cream	1 teaspoonful vanilla

Soak gelatin in coffee. Scald milk then add I cupful sugar, salt and well-beaten yolks. Cool and fold in cream whipped with vanilla and teaspoonful sugar, and egg whites beaten stiff.
Frances P. Rudolph   *Southern Delight* 1923

Tennessee Woman Suffrage Heritage Trail

http://tnwomansuffrageheritagetrail.com

The Perfect 36 – When Tennessee Delivered Suffrage

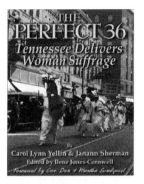

That it happened in Tennessee — when no other state was close — is a source of immense pride. The story of Woman Suffrage is inspiring. We hope you cherish your right to vote and will visit many of the sites on this heritage trail and support adding Clarksville's Tennessee Triumph.

Knoxville Statue representing

East - Lizzie Crozier French

Middle – Anne Dallas Dudley

West – Elizabeth Avery Meriwether

Knoxville Statue of

Mother and son

Phebb and Harry Burn

Jackson Statue of

Sue Shelton White

Nashville Statue in Centennial Park

Carrie Chapman Catt – National

Anne Dallas Dudley - Nashville

Frankie Pierce – Smith County

Sue Shelton White - Jackson

Abby Crawford Milton - Chattanooga

Clarksville Statue

Tennessee Triumph represents the women of Clarksville who worked for Suffrage steadfastly year after year, not famous or rewarded, except by the successful achievement of their goal. We honor their commitment and laud their perseverance.

August 2018 Equality Day Celebration in Centennial Park

Commemorative public art projects are underway
in Chattanooga and Memphis also

Contributed Recipes 2018

Beverages

Celebrating Women's Equality Day in Centennial Park at the unveiling of the Woman's Suffrage Statue, promoted by the Yellow Rose Society headed up by Paula Casey in 2016. Casey was a reporter for The Leaf-Chronicle for many years, including 1990 when we celebrated the 75th Anniversary. Pictured left to right, Barbara Beeman, Debby Johnson and Dee Boaz.

Boiled Custard

½ gallon milk   6 eggs, separated
1 ½ cups sugar   1 tsp. vanilla

Heat milk in double boiler. In large mixing bowl, beat egg yolks and add sugar gradually. Beat egg whites and add gradually to egg yolk mixture, beating thoroughly. Add about 1 cup milk to this mixture and mix well. Add to remaining hot milk in double boiler, stirring constantly. Cook and stir until foam disappears or mixture begins to thicken. Add vanilla.

Submitted by Betty Cole. In honor of her mother Lois O'Reilly Nichols. Lois was an exceptional seamstress. She was a member of the Home Demonstration Club (now known as FCE) and an early member of the Beachaven Garden Club. At flower shows, she won many blue ribbons for her horticulture specimens and her flower arrangements.

Mariel's Boiled Custard

2 quarts sweet milk   1 Tsp. vanilla
4 heaping Tsp. flour   4 eggs
1 cup sugar

Scald milk in top of a double boiler. Mix flour with sugar. Separate eggs and beat yolks until fluffy. Add sugar and flour to egg yolk mixture and mix thoroughly. Add small amount of scalded milk to egg mixture and then slowly add the mixture to the scalded milk. Stir well and cook until the mixture gets to desired custard thickness, stirring frequently.

Beat the egg whites until stiff. Remove the thickened custard from heat and fold in the egg whites. Cool. Add flavoring and put in refrigerator to cool.
Submitted by Mary Moore. In honor of her mother Mariel Thompson.

"Methodist" Fruit Tea

6 tea bags
4 cups boiling water
1 ¼ cup sugar
1 (6 oz.) can frozen orange juice, thawed
1 (6 oz.) can frozen lemonade, thawed
10 cups cold water
Steep tea bags in boiling water 5 minutes. Discard tea bags. Dissolve sugar in hot tea. Add juices and cold water to the mixture in a 1 gallon container. Serves 16.

Submitted by Ann S. Clark. This tea was served at a luncheon many years ago at Madison Street United Methodist Church. A Presbyterian friend, who had attended, requested the recipe. She referred to it as that "Methodist Tea."

Plantation Mint Tea

1 quart boiling water
2 bags plantation mint tea
1 cup sugar
6 oz. can frozen lemonade
4 (6 oz) cans water
1 ½ cups pineapple juice
Pour boiling water over sugar and tea bags; steep for 30 minutes. Remove tea bags. Add lemonade, water, and pineapple juice. Mix. Makes about 2 ½ quarts. Pour over ice in glass to serve.

Submitted by Barbara Nichols Collier. Barbara is an avid gardener and a Master Gardener in Dyersburg, TN. She is in the hand bell choir at her church, a member of the garden club, and in a music club. Her gardening articles have been published in the State Gazette of Dyersburg.

"Drink Water Campaign"

Raspberry Lime Fiesta Water Recipe
Quarter 2 limes squeeze the juice and add limes to pitcher.
Add Raspberries. Press lightly to release some of the juices. Fill with ice and then add water to the top. Stir, cover and refrigerate.

Pineapple Kiwi Breeze
1/4th pineapple peeled and cut into triangle peeled and cut into triangles.
1 kiwi peeled and sliced. Add water and ice, refrigerate

Watermelon-Mint Splash Water Recipe
Add a sprig of mint to pitcher and muddle gently.
Add watermelon cubes; press gently to release juices. Fill pitcher with ice cubes, add water to the top, stir, cover and refrigerate.

Submitted by Family Consumer Science Agent Tamera Adjei. The Drinking Water Campaign is the *"University of TN and TN State University campaign to replace sugary drinks with flavored water."* Tamera started work at Extension as Nutrition Educator in 2010. In 2017 she was officially named FCE Agent for UT Extension of Montgomery County.

Pink Tu-Tu Punch
1 qt. cranberry juice cocktail, chilled
1 to 1½ cups sugar
1 qt. pineapple juice chilled
2 qts. Ginger ale chilled
Combine all ingredients: stir well. Serve over ice.
Yields 1 gallon.

Submitted by Pat Woods.

A "knock-out" Punch
4 liters Seven-Up
1 to 2 large cans HI-C orange drink (to taste)
1 12 oz. can Apricot nectar juice
1 to 2 qts. Rainbow sherbet (to taste)
Freeze **whole** oranges, lemons, limes
Chill all liquids.
Combine all liquids in the punch bowl and add sherbet. Add whole or slice the frozen fruits and add to punch. Stir gently letting sherbet melt slightly.
Yield: About 16 cups.

Submitted by Pat Woods

"Yellow Rose" Holiday Tea Punch
3 cups boiling water	1¼ cups fresh orange juice
10 tea bags (black tea)	3 cups sugar
24 whole cloves	4 qts. cold water
1 3inch cinnamon stick, crumbled	Orange Slices
2¼ cups fresh lemon juice	Lemon slices

Pour boiling water over tea bags, whole cloves, and crumbled stick cinnamon sticks. Cover and steep 5 minutes.
Strain (with cheese cloth preferably) and let cool.
Add lemon juice, orange juice and sugar stirring until the sugar is dissolved.
Add cold water.
Pour into punch bowl with an ice ring or ice cubes.
Garnish with orange and lemon slices.
Yield: about 50 (four ounce) servings.

Submitted by Pat Woods.

Tummy Warmer Punch
1 bottle (1 pint) light corn syrup
1-gallon apple cider or apple juice
1 can (46 ounces) pineapple juice
1 can (6 ounces) frozen lemonade concentrate
 A big pot!
Mix together corn syrup, pineapple juice, cider, and lemonade concentrate in a large pot. Bring to a boil. Keep warm in a crock pot. Serve hot.
Yields 32 - three quarter cup servings.

Submitted by Pat Woods.

Mocha Punch (16 servings)
¼ cup instant coffee   4 cups water
½ cup Ghirardelli dark chocolate syrup   4 cups (1 quart) milk
1 quart vanilla ice cream
Use enough hot water to dissolve coffee and finish with cold.
Mix liquid coffee & syrup. Chill overnight
Add milk and serve over ice cream or combine in punch bowl.

Submitted by Barbara Brown Beeman.

Agua Fresca
1 small cucumber, organic scrubbed and sliced
2 sprigs of fresh mint washed and bruised
½ lime organic scrubbed and sliced, optional but very tasty. If kept more than a day, remove the lime or the water will become bitter.
10 to 12 cups of filtered water
Place sliced cucumber, mint sprigs and lime slices in a large pitcher.
Pour water into pitcher, cover and refrigerate for 1 to 8 hours.
The longer you infuse the stronger the flavor.
Strain into glasses and garnish with a slice of cucumber.
This is a definite cooling and thirst-quenching drink for summer!

Submitted by Pat Woods.

Punch

Punch comes from the Indian word **Panch** which means five. Punch was introduced to the United Kingdom from India in the early seventeenth century.

Old Caribbean Punch Rhyme

"One of sour
Two of sweet
Three of strong
Four of weak"

Sour – one measure lime juice
Sweet – two measures of sugar/sugar syrup
Strong – three parts Dark Rum (leave out for children)
Weak – four parts water or passion fruit juice, but reduce the sugar
Also, use black tea and spices

A measure or part equaled one pint.

Punch Cups

Most punch cups, glass or plastic, hold 4 ounces. A recipe that makes 160 ounces of punch will provide 40 servings. If you have 20 guests and plan on one to two servings per guests, you have the perfect recipe.
160 ounces also = about 20 8-ounce cups.

Ice Ring

You will need a mold, fruit slices like peach slices, seedless grapes, strawberry halves, or orange slices. Whatever your preference. You can also use herbs for greenery. Mint works nicely. Think about the flavor of your punch.

Rinse a ring mold (or whatever you are using for a mold) with cold water.
Place in the freezer for 30 minutes. Remove and pour in cold water to a depth of ¼ inch.
Arrange the fruit pieces in a pattern in the water.
Freeze for 1 hour. When frozen carefully fill mold with cold water and freeze until solid. This may take several hours. Or freeze overnight.

If prepared the day before cover mold with plastic wrap after it is frozen so it doesn't take on odors.
To unmold, dip into warm water, invert on a plate and carefully lift and slide mold into the punch.

Appetizers

Trees of Christmas 2016
Smith Trahern Mansion

"Tennessee Sin" Dip

8 oz. cream cheese
8 oz. sour cream
2 cups shredded cheese (I like medium or sharp)
1 cup cooked ham chopped fine (deli ham works fine)
1 cup green onions sliced thin (I add green tops)
¼ tsp. Worcestershire sauce (or more if desired)
¼ cup red pepper chopped fine (nice color but can be omitted)

Mix cream cheese and sour cream until smooth. Add remaining ingredients and mix well. Put in lightly buttered 1 quart casserole dish and cover with foil. Place in preheated 350 degree oven and baked covered for 30 minutes. Serve in chafing dish, if possible, to keep warm. Arrange plain bagel slices on one side of a serving platter. Arrange carrot sticks, celery, bell pepper strips (red, green, yellow) to fill platter.

Submitted by Nancy Glass Hancock. I grew up in an era when our vegetables were homegrown and most meals were prepared "from scratch." The kitchen was large and full of sunlight and happy conversation. Ours was a three-generation home. In addition to my parents and me, my grandmother was an important part of our home. I still love using the wonderful cast-iron skillets and Dutch ovens that were my grandmother's favorites in the kitchen. As my life became busier with marriage, two daughters, pets, and a university teaching career, I gradually moved away from the "scratch" prepared meals of my childhood. Now I depend on "store-bought" ingredients that take much less time to prepare and to have table ready. "Tennessee Sin" is one of my favorite appetizers—not original with me but something I love to serve to guests.

Chinese Fried Walnuts

4 cups shelled walnuts

Vegetable oil

½ cup sugar

1/8 teaspoon salt

In a large saucepan over high heat, heat 6 cups water to boiling. Add walnuts and reheat to boiling. Cook 1 minute. Rinse under running hot water and drain. In large bowl toss walnuts in sugar. In deep skillet heat about 1-inch oil to 350 degrees. With slotted spoon add about half walnuts to oil and fry for 5 minutes or until golden, stirring often. With slotted spoon place walnuts in colander over bowl to drain. Sprinkle with salt. Toss lightly to cool. Do same with remaining walnuts. Store in tightly covered containers.

Submitted by Hillwood Club. In honor Velma "Pete" Ackley---Velma "Pete" was a retired nurse from Ft. Campbell, KY who joined Hillwood, also spoke to class at APSU on Health Aspects of aging Diseases.

Hot and Sassy Sausage Pin Wheels

1 pkg. refrigerated crescent roll dough

½ pound of hot sausage

½ pound of mild or sage sausage

Preheat oven to 375°. Place crescent dough onto a baking sheet, press into a 14x10-inch rectangle. Combine sausages together in small mixing bowl. Spread sausage almost to the edge of the dough. Roll up jelly roll fashion and slice ½ inch thick. Place pinwheels on baking sheet. Bake until golden brown and sausage is cooked through, 12-16 minutes.

Submitted by Martha Martin Pile. This is a Christmas favorite at Smith Trahern Mansion. When my daughter Vicky was living in a hotel, waiting for her new house to be finished, she needed to have a dish for church events. She just got to church early and made this no mess special.

Cheese Cookies
½ cup Butter
2 cups sharp cheese
1 cup flour
½ tsp. coarse ground black pepper
1 tsp. salt (I prefer seasoned salt)
Cream butter and cheese, add other ingredients and cream all
together well. Roll into long ropes, the size you want your cookies to
be. Refrigerate until firm. Slice into rounds and bake in a preheated
oven at 325 degrees for 20 minutes.
(Roll on a floured surface then roll up in waxed paper before placing
in the refrigerator. This makes them easier to handle.

Submitted by Patsy Sharpe. Over 40 years ago, a friend served these
cookies at a Home Interiors party and I begged for her recipe. I have
tweaked it some to make it my own.

Cheese Straws
1 lb. New York sharp cheese   ¼ tsp. paprika
1 stick butter   ¼ tsp. Worcestershire sauce
2 cups flour   1 tsp. salt or celery salt
¼ tsp. red pepper
Grate cheese. Let cheese and butter stand until room temperature.
Squeeze with hands to mix. Add Worcestershire sauce. Combine
with dry ingredients. (Makes a stiff dough.) Using a cookie press with
star design, form long lines on cookie sheets. Bake at 300 degree
oven for 20 to 25 minutes or until firm to touch. Break into 2 to 3
inch pieces. Store in covered container.

Submitted by Betty Nichols Cole. In honor of grandmother Ora
O'Reilly. Ora was an accomplished seamstress and artist. I remember
her at her treadle machine sewing dance recital costumes. Then at
age 65, she began china painting. In 1973 at age 81, she painted for
me a teapot, four cups and saucers and four dessert plates with a
lovely yellow rose pattern.

Olive Cheese Porcupine
4 oz blue cheese
1 tsp. Worcestershire sauce
8 oz cream cheese
½ cup finely chopped walnuts
1 lb sharp cheddar cheese,
Shredded Parsley, chopped or dry
1 T minced onion
 Spanish green olives
Allow cheese to soften. Mix with remaining ingredients, except olives. Form mixture into egg shape. Refrigerate or freeze at least 2 hours. Roll in paprika and let stand 1/2 hour before serving. Garnish with olives on wooden picks for "quills". Use half an olive for each eye. Serve with crisp crackers.

Submitted by Barbara Brown Beeman. Barbara first served this dish to her classes at Lafayette High School, Lexington KY, in early 60's. Barbara is the president elect for Western Region Family and Communication and has been involved at the State National Country Women of the World.

Zucchini Appetizers

4 eggs, slightly beaten	2 Tbs. snipped parsley
½ cup vegetable oil	½ cup Parmesan cheese
1 clove garlic, finely chopped	3 cups thinly sliced zucchini
Dash pepper	1 cup Bisquick
1 tsp. marjoram or oregano	½ tsp. salt
½ tsp seasoned salt	½ cup onions, finely chopped

Heat oven to 350 degrees. Grease oblong 13x9x2 inch pan. Bake 25 to 30 minutes, until golden brown. Cut into 2 x 1 inch pieces. Makes 4 doz. Triangles.

Submitted by Beverly Nichols Ball.

Korean Sesame Fried Chicken Wings

Crisco oil, for frying
8 cloves garlic minced
1 (1½-inch) piece ginger, peeled & grated finely
6-7 stalks of chopped green onions
3 tbsp. soy sauce
1 tablespoon sesame seeds
½ teaspoon garlic powder
3 tbsp. gojujang (Korean chili paste) OPTIONAL
1½ tbsp. rice vinegar
1 tbsp. Asian sesame oil
1 tbsp. honey
⅔ cup flour
1 tbsp. cornstarch
16 chicken wings (about 2 lbs.)

Pour oil into a 6-qt. pot to a depth of 2 inches. Heat over medium-high heat until a thermometer reads 350˚. Chop garlic and ginger in a food processor or a grater. Add soy sauce, gojujang, vinegar, sesame oil, sesame seeds, green onion, and honey; puree. Put sauce into a bowl. Whisk flour, cornstarch, garlic powder, and ⅔ cup water in another bowl. Add chicken; toss until well coated in batter. Working in 3 batches, fry chicken until golden, 8-10 minutes. Drain on paper towels. Return oil to 350˚ between batches. Toss fried wings in sauce to thoroughly coat. Serve with white rice. (4 servings)

Submitted by Susan White. Susan is known for her great cooking and enjoys most being a mother. Pat Woods says "she is my favorite daughter-in-law."

Benedictine Sandwich Spread

8 ounces cream cheese	2 Tbs. red onion, finely chopped
¼ tsp. kosher salt	1/8 tsp. red pepper

1 cucumber, peeled, seeded, finely chopped, juice drained and discarded

Bring cream cheese to room temperature. Add other ingredients and mix well.

Submitted by Rubye Patch. In honor of Lily Bell Sewell Trahern (1874-1962). Lily Bell Trahern was born in Louisville and moved to Anchorage, KY in 1880. At Miss Belle Peers' Girls' School, Lily Bell met Clarksville's Nettie Turnley (Wade), who introduced her to Elwyn Baxter Trahern, whom she married in 1897. In 1911, the Traherns purchased the antebellum TIP TOP, a "sister" home of the Smith/Trahern Mansion, as both are thought to have been designed by the Prussian architect, Adolphus Heiman. Miss Jennie Benedict opened a tea room in Louisville. This is one of Miss Jennie's famous recipes which Lily Belle brought with her to Clarksville.

Tuna Crunch

1 pkg. wonton wrappers	8 oz. low-fat cream cheese
1 tsp curry powder	2 tsp Worcestershire sauce
½ cup finely chopped onion	2 ribs celery chopped
6 oz. tuna rinsed twice	3 oz. broccoli slaw or rainbow salad

Soften cream cheese and add remaining ingredients, refrigerate until ready to use. Separate wontons into squares and place in mini muffin pans. Bake 5 minutes at 350. Baked wontons will keep at room temperature until ready to serve. Fill each wonton with tuna mixture. Filled wontons will soften if prepared far in advance.

Submitted by Barbara Brown Beeman. Barbara served this dish at Christmas Open House in 2000 and at first NAFCE members reception at 2005 TAFCE conference in Kingsport, when she was state president.

salads

2018 Training everywhere the Suffragist went and lived the Tour Guides were sure to follow

Greek Chicken Salad
This recipe starts with a chicken from Sam's or Costco so it comes together fast. Also, I love that it is a not mayonnaise based.
¾ Cup Greek yogurt (any fat % you want to use)
2 Tbs. fresh lemon juice
3 cloves of garlic minced or pressed
1 medium seedless cucumber chopped
4 cups of shredded rotisserie chicken
6-8 grape or cherry tomatoes quartered
½ a medium purple onion chopped
4 oz feta cheese crumbled
¼ Cup Kalamata olives chopped
2 Tbs. fresh dill chopped
2 Tbs. parsley chopped
Salt and pepper to taste
In a large bowl combine all of the ingredients, mix well. Chill until ready to serve with pita bread.

Submitted by Sandy Brennan.

Everlasting Slaw
1 medium head cabbage, grated
1 medium onion, chopped
1 medium pepper, chopped
Bring to boil:
1 cup sugar   ¼ tsp turmeric
1 cup vinegar   1 tsp celery seed
Salt and pepper to taste
Pour over cabbage mixture while still hot. Refrigerate at least overnight. Stirring often will keep in refrigerator for several days.

Submitted by Mary Moore in honor of her mother Mariel Thompson.

Chicken Tomato Cucumber Salad
Combine:
½ cup small diced onions
2 cups medium diced cucumber (peeled in strips)
2 cups medium diced tomatoes
2 cups medium diced cooked chicken breast
½ cup rough chopped cilantro
3 Tbs. olive oil
Toss together, cover, and refrigerator. Just before serving, add salt to taste and juice of 2 lemons. Simple and good!

Submitted by Linda R. Nichols
In 1960, I did a radio interview with Alma Reece, the first female VP of old Northern Bank on the corner of N. 2nd and Main. In 1962, I was told by the realtor that I was the first unmarried female in the southeastern United States to buy a house in my own name, without a man to sign the FHA mortgage with me.

Broccoli Salad
1 bunch broccoli, chopped
2 cup shredded cheese
1/3 onion, chopped
6-8 slices of bacon, crumbled
1/3 box golden raisins
Dressing:
1 cup mayonnaise
2 Tbs. vinegar
1/4 cup sugar
Mix together salad ingredients. Combine dressing ingredients and pour over salad.

Submitted by Chrissie Brown. Chrissie is a member of Hillwood FCE, a working mom who helps with special events. Her son Jackson attended club meetings with his grandmother Barbara Brown from 6 weeks old until he started school!

Elizabeth's Awesome Pasta Salad

Dressing:

1 cup vegetable oil
½ cup grated Parmesan cheese
¼ cup white wine vinegar
½ tsp. pepper
¼ tsp. fresh basil
2 minced garlic cloves
3 Tbs. sugar

Salad:

10 oz. bag fresh spinach
2 cup cooked bowtie pasta
1½ cup cooked crumbled bacon
½ cup chopped green onion
2 c. shredded mozzarella cheese
¾ cup shredded cheddar cheese

Combine dressing and pour over salad.
This makes a very large salad and can be refrigerated for 4 days.

Submitted by Beverly Parker. As a past president of FCE, I know firsthand the contributions this talented group of women has made in Clarksville-Montgomery County. The FCE, without doubt, has supported the efforts of women more than any other entity in this area.

Old Fashioned Potato Salad

6 large potatoes
celery (optional)
small jar of Pimentos
2 eggs (optional)
salt and pepper to taste

½ cup carrots
1 cup mayonnaise
green pepper
onion

Boil potatoes in the skins. Peel potatoes after cooking thoroughly.
Add pimentos, grated carrots, chopped onion, and mayonnaise.
Season with salt and pepper.
Optional: mix finely chopped egg with the mayo before mixing in salad and add chopped celery and green pepper.

Submitted by Shirley Winn. In memory of her mother-in-law Carolyn Mayhew Jackson (1919-2016.) Carolyn was a great lady. She loved her 4 boys and was extremely active in her church all the years that I knew her. She worked tirelessly to quilt for Project Linus, teach her Sunbeam Girls, and put together cookbooks. She never met a stranger and everyone called her Granny.

Campanelle Pasta Salad

1 pound campanelle pasta	¼ c. extra-virgin olive oil + ¼ cup
1 small med. red onion, chopped	2 cloves garlic, minced
1 6 oz. can tuna in oil, drained	2 cups cherry tomatoes halved
2 Tbs. capers, rinsed and drained	2 Tbs. chopped fresh thyme

¼ cup chopped fresh parsley
8 oz. frozen artichoke hearts, thawed quartered
Kosher salt and freshly ground pepper

Bring a large pot of salted water to boil over high heat. Add the pasta and cook until tender but still firm, about 8 to 10 minutes. Drain and reserve 1 cup pasta water. In a 14 inch skillet, heat ¼ cup of oil over medium high heat. Add onion and cook, stirring frequently, until soft (about 5 minutes). Add garlic and cook about 30 seconds until aromatic. Add tuna to skillet and break into chunks with a fork. Add cherry tomatoes, artichoke hearts, capers, and thyme. Cook, stirring occasionally, until tomatoes begin to soften, about 8 to 10 minutes. Add pasta, remaining ¼ cup of oil, and parsley. Toss until all ingredients are coated, adding a little pasta water if needed to thin out the sauce. Season with salt and pepper to taste. Serve warm or room temperature.

Submitted by Marsha Green.

Momma's Salad

Red grapes, red apples, walnuts, miniature marshmallows, whipped crème or Cool Whip. Cut grapes in half lengthwise. Chop unpeeled, cored apples in bite size pieces. Combine all ingredients then fold in whipped cream and chill well before serving.

Submitted by Sherry Wingfield. This salad was passed down to me from my mother Nadine Wingfield and was served at every family occasion. I have continued the tradition and passed this salad to my daughter-in-law and now even my grandchildren are learning to prepare it.

Spinach Artichoke Pasta Salad
Coarse salt
1 Package tortellini (fresh mushroom, chicken prosciutto or spinach)
½ pound fresh baby spinach
1 roasted red pepper drained and chopped
1 (15 ounce) can baby artichoke hearts in water drained and chopped
½ small red onion chopped
1 clove garlic
1 lemon zest
2 tsp. lemon juice + the juice of one wedge
2 tbs. red wine vinegar + a couple of splashes
¼ cup of extra virgin olive oil
1 tbs. fresh thyme leaves, chopped (or ½ teaspoon dried)
Black pepper
Handful of sun dried tomatoes packed in oil coarsely chopped
Bring 5 or 6 inches of water to a boil in a large pot. Salt boiling water and add pasta. Cook for 3 to 4 minutes until just tender and the tortellini are floating. Drain tortellini then cool by spreading them in a single layer on a large plate or cookie sheet. Coarsely chop baby spinach. Combine with chopped artichokes, roasted red pepper and red onion. Chop Garlic, add salt and mash into a paste with the flat of your knife. Transfer garlic paste to a small bowl and add lemon zest, lemon juice and vinegar. Whisk in oil, thyme and pepper. Add pasta and sundried tomatoes to the salad dress and gently toss. Serve or refrigerate.

Submitted by Jennifer Britton. I live in Chesapeake, Virginia and have 2 children. I am a sales manager at a hotel in Norfolk, Virginia. I volunteered with Martha Pile at the Smith-Trahern Mansion the summer of 1999.

Honey Walnut Fruit Salad

1/3 cup honey	½ cup light mayonnaise
½ cup chopped walnuts	2 apples cored
2 sliced bananas	1 cup seedless grapes
11 oz. mandarin oranges drained	1 tbs. lemon juice
1 cup shredded lettuce	

Blend honey and mayonnaise until smooth.
Toss Remaining ingredients with lemon juice. Stir in honey mixture.
Refrigerate.

Submitted by Marie Cross. Marie and her sister Frances Hatcher were invited to join FCE by Martha Pile after she attended their family reunion. Marie was not known to cook—she left that to her sister.

Cherry Salad

2 small pkgs. cherry Jell-O
2 cups hot water
1 #2can crushed pineapple (do not drain)
1 #2 can cherry pie filling
1 cup chopped nuts
Dissolve Jell-O in hot water. Add other ingredients.
Refrigerate until gelatin sets.

Topping:

1 8 oz. pkg. cream cheese
1 8 oz. sour cream
1/2 cup sugar
1 tsp. vanilla
1 cup chopped nuts
Mix cream cheese and sour cream. Add sugar, vanilla and beat until it forms stiff peaks. Spread over Jell-O mixture.
After it has set, sprinkle with chopped nuts.

Submitted by Eleanor Duncan.

Coca-Cola Salad

1 (3 oz.) package raspberry Jell-O   1 (3 oz.) package cherry Jell-O
1 14 ounce can crushed pineapple   2 cans dark sweet cherries
1 8 ounce block cream cheese   3 cups reserved juice
2 cans Coke, Diet Coke, Cherry Coke, or Diet Cherry Coke

Drain the crushed pineapple and dark sweet cherries through a strainer into a glass measuring cup. Add enough water to make 3 cups liquid. Heat until boiling. Pour into a large bowl, add the 2 packages of Jell-O and stir until well-dissolved. Pour into 13 x 9 dish. Add the cream cheese, separating and mashing with a fork until in small pieces. Add the drained crushed pineapple and dark sweet cherries. Distribute evenly and put into refrigerator to chill.
After about one hour, add the 2 cans of Coke. Distribute evenly. Skim off foam with metal spoon. Return to refrigerator.
Chill for at least 8 hours or until well-congealed.

Submitted by Leslie Henson.

Frosted Cranberry Jell-O Salad

1 (13½ oz.) can crushed pineapple   2 (3 oz.) package Lemon Jell-O
7 oz. Ginger ale   8 oz. cream cheese
1 (1 pound) can whole cranberry sauce
1 (2 oz.) package Dream Whip
½ cup chopped pecans

Drain pineapple, reserving juice. Add water to make 1 cup. Boil; add Jell-O stirring to dissolve. Slowly stir in ginger ale. Blend pineapple and cranberry sauce. Fold into Jell-O. Chill in 9x9 inch dish. Make Dream Whip according package directions. Beat in cream cheese. Spread over Jell-O and top with pecans. (May substitute Dream Whip package with a tub of Cool Whip and beat in cream cheese)

Submitted by Carol Shawver. I have lived in Clarksville for 7 years. I enjoy spending time with my granddaughter Haley, who lives in Clarksville. I enjoy cooking and I bake for the Sweetheart Cake Bake every year.

Breads

The Smith Trahern Mansion is named for Lucy and Christopher Smith who built the home in 1858 and Margaret and Joe Trahern who restored the home in the late 1940s and son Joseph Trahern who lived here. Pictured are Joseph Trahern and Debby Johnson.

Aunt Lucille's Refrigerator Rolls

2 yeast cakes	1 cup ice water
2 eggs beaten	5 cups flour
1 tsp. salt	¾ lard
½ cup sugar	½ cup sugar
1 cup boiling water	

Dissolve yeast cakes in ice water. Cream the sugar, lard and salt. Pour the boiling water over this mixture, cool to lukewarm. Add eggs, then yeast. Add flour slowly. Cover and let rise. This will keep 3-4 days in the refrigerator. Knead several times on a floured board.
Bake in 450-degree oven until golden brown.

Submitted Jacqueline Crouch. This recipe is one that defines comfort food for me. We embraced these as warmly as her stories, laughter, and gifts.

Egg Twist Bread

Add dry yeast to ¼ cup water	2 Tbsp. Oil
2 Tbsp. Honey	3 eggs
2 tsp salt	4½ - 6 cups flour

Add above ingredients and beat in flour, making a sticky dough. Turn on floured board and knead, adding up to 6 c. flour. Smooth, elastic dough (knead 10 minutes or so).Let rise in greased bowl--oil all sides-- 1 1/2 hours. Cover with towel. Punch down, flip over, cover, let rise 5 minutes. Divide into 3 equal balls, roll each into long roll, braid, let rise in greased pan 1 1/2 hours or until double. Brush top with beaten egg and sprinkle with poppy or sesame seeds. Bake at 350° for 40 minutes.

Submitted by Hillwood FCE. In honor of Penny Darnell, wife of Riley Darnell Sec of State, early member Hillwood FCE.

Alice's Egg Bread
Heat skillet with 3 Tbs. oil in 400 degree oven
Mix: 1½ cups buttermilk   1 or 2 eggs
          2 tsp. baking powder   ¼ to ½ tsp. soda
Meal--- (Just experiment. Best not to get too thick.) Salt to taste.

Submitted by Chris Crow. In honor of Alice Neblett Dinsmore (1917-2018).

Ella's Perfect Cornbread
1 ½ cup Martha White self-rising corn meal
½ cup Martha White self-rising flour (don't sift)
1 ¾ cup buttermilk
1 egg (beaten)
¼ cup Mazola corn oil
Preheat oven to 425° oven. Mix corn meal, flour, buttermilk and egg together, set aside.
Put corn oil in a seasoned skillet (iron or other) and heat for 4-5 minute in 425° oven. Pour hot oil into the corn meal mixture—stir a few times. Pour mixture into the hot skillet.
Cook bread at 425° for 22-26 minutes (don't let bread get too brown on top). Remove from oven and run a spatula or knife around the edges of the skillet and underneath the bread. Turn bread onto plate; slice, butter and serve.

Submitted by Suella Arrington. In honor of Ella McCurdy Dillard. Ella (born 1920) would have marched for woman's suffrage had she been born sooner. A schoolteacher for 27 years, she was a feisty independent woman.

Delinia's Cornbread
1 cup self-rising corn meal   2 eggs
½ cup cooking oil   ½ cup cream style corn
1 cup (8oz.) sour cream
Mix well and bake at 400 degrees for 20-25 min.
Bake in 8 or 9inch pan or iron skillet.

Submitted by Delinia Storr.

Mexican Cornbread

2 Cups self-rising cornmeal
¼ tsp. soda
½ tsp salt
1 ½ tsp crushed red pepper
1 cup grated sharp cheddar cheese

2 beaten eggs
½ cup oil
1 cup buttermilk
1 cup cream style corn

Blend dry ingredients. Add eggs, oil, and buttermilk. Mix well. Add corn and cheese. Preheat oven to 450 degrees; add 1-2 tbs. oil in iron skillet, put in oven to heat. Bake 15-20 minutes, until brown on top.

Submitted by Harriet Tate. Harriet Tate was born and raised in Montgomery County and will be 102 on January 2, 2019. She has 4 grown daughters, 8 grandchildren, and 17 great grandchildren. She loves to cook and has baked for the Sweetheart Cake Bake for many years.

Cheese and Bacon Muffins

2 cups sifted flour
2 ½ tsp. Baking Powder
¾ teaspoon Salt
1 teaspoon Sugar
½ cup unsalted butter

1 ¼ cup shredded mild cheddar cheese
9 slices bacon fried and crumbled
1 egg well beaten
1 cup milk

First fry your bacon and set aside to cool. Cool and crumble. Sift flour, baking powder, sugar and salt into a large bowl together. Stir. Cut butter into flour mixture. Add the crumbled bacon, cheddar cheese, and mix. Pour milk into well beaten egg. Mix with flour-bacon-cheese mixture until all ingredients are moistened. Spoon this mixture into a 12-cup large greased muffin pan. Bake in 400°F Oven for 25 minutes. Makes 12 muffins. Freezes well.

Submitted by Renate Hernandez.

Grandma Ethel Feather's Banana Bread

1 cup sugar	1 cup butter
2 eggs	3 bananas mashed
2 cups flour	1 teaspoon baking soda
½ cup nuts	

Cream sugar and butter. Add eggs and Bananas.
Sift together flour and soda and add to mixture add nuts if desired.
Beat Well.
Bake 1 hour 350 degrees in greased/floured loaf pan.

Submitted by Hillwood Club. In honor of Eleanor Felts. Eleanor was first member willing to follow in Nancy Neal's footsteps as club president. When NAFCE was in Oregon, Eleanor sent money to her brother, Tad Feather, to rent a car to drive Nancy Neal, Peggy Roddy, and Barbara Brown to tour the countryside. Her memorial service was held at the Smith-Trahern Mansion.

Whole Wheat Banana (Nut) Bread

5 overly ripe bananas	2 tsp. baking soda
3 eggs	3 cups whole wheat flour
1 tsp vanilla	1 cup chopped nuts
¾ cup margarine	
1 ½ cups sugar	

Liquefy bananas, eggs, vanilla, margarine, and sugar in a blender. Pour into mixing bowl. Add soda, flour, and nuts (if using) and mix thoroughly. Pour into 1 greased 10" tube or Bundt pan. Bake at 350° for 45 to 55 minutes, until cake tester inserted into the center comes out clean.

Submitted by Donna Wilson. Donna teaches the rights and responsibilities of citizenship to immigrants on their pathway to becoming U.S. citizens. She is proud to wear her "I Voted" sticker on Election Day.

Nilla Nut Muffins

½ lb. margarine

2 c. sugar

6 whole eggs, room temperature

11 oz. box vanilla wafers crushed

½ cup milk

11 oz. shredded coconut

1 cup chopped nuts

Cream margarine and sugar together. Add eggs, one at a time. Alternate adding crushed wafers and milk. Add coconut and pecans. Pour into lined muffin cups and bake at 300° for 20-25 minutes until toothpick inserted comes out clean.

Submitted by Hillwood FCE in honor of Linda Edington. Linda, a member of Hillwood, shared her mother's muffin recipe which is a staple at The Looking Glass Restaurant and Bakery, which she owned. She was also very active in Garden Club and environmental issues. She chaired the Trees of Christmas for three years and was always generous with her time and talents.

Harvest Apple French Toast

12.5oz. pkgs. frozen French toast, thawed

1 ½ cups milk or half and half

9 eggs, lightly beaten

3 medium red baking apples

¾ cup walnuts, chopped

½ cup pancake syrup

2 tsp. cinnamon

½ cup brown sugar

4 tbs. butter

¾ cup Craisins or raisins

Powdered sugar and additional syrup for garnish

Cut French toast into 1" cubes and place in bottom of greased 4 quart casserole; mix milk and eggs and pour over toast, stirring gently to coat. Core and slice apples; chop walnuts, sauté apples, walnuts, syrup, cinnamon and brown sugar in 4 T butter for about 5 minutes or until apples are crisp tender; pour apple mixture over toast and sprinkle with Craisins. Cover and refrigerate overnight; bake covered @ 375° for 40 minutes; remove cover and bake additional 5 minutes; let stand for 5 minutes and sprinkle with powdered sugar and additional syrup before serving.

Submitted by Alice Pitts. Alice is a Belmont FCE member, County Council officer, and mother of our newly elected city mayor, Joe Pitts.

Oven French Toast

3 Large eggs	¾ cup whole milk
1 tablespoon white sugar	¼ teaspoon salt
¼ teaspoon ground cinnamon	¼ teaspoon nutmeg

8 slices bread (white, raisin, or cinnamon)

2 tablespoons salted butter

Crack eggs into large, flat bowl. Beat them with a fork or wire whisk. Add milk and mix. Add sugar and salt. Sprinkle in cinnamon and nutmeg. Mix everything up thoroughly with the fork. Place salted butter in 9x13 inch baking pan. Stick it in the preheated oven for 1 minute. Remove pan from oven. Quickly, dip each slice of bread in the batter mixture, flip it over to coat the other side. Place it in the hot buttered pan, scrunching all 8 battered slices together in the pan. Pour any remaining batter evenly over the slices in the pan. Bake in the oven until the bottoms are browned, this usually takes about 5 to 8 minutes. (Check by lifting edge with a fork.)

Once the bottoms have browned, flip them over with a fork and bake them for 2 to 4 minutes longer or until the tops are golden brown. Remove pan from oven and cover with foil until ready to serve. Serve with butter, syrup, or jam. Yield: 8 one-piece servings or 4 two-piece servings. (This recipe can be cooked on the stove-top burner. Heating burner to medium-high, dip bread in batter the fry it on both sides.)

Submitted by Betty J. Davis. I fell in love with the Smith-Trahern Mansion and its tall ceilings, and beautiful chandelier on my first visit in 1999. To help with its up keep, I have baked and donated many cakes for the Valentine's Day fundraiser. Some of my granddaughters' first memories of Christmas with "Grammie" include a visit to the mansion during the Trees of Christmas. Whenever I have visitors from out of town, I always bring them to tour the Smith-Trahern mansion. As with me, Clarksville wouldn't be the same without the Smith-Trahern Mansion as a part of its living history.

High Fiber Omega 3 Bread

Mix all dry ingredients together:

> 1 Cup Organic Rye Flour
> 5 Cups Organic Unbleached All-Purpose Flour
> 2 teaspoon Salt
> 3 Tablespoons Gluten
> 2 Tablespoons Barley Flour
> 2 Tablespoons Oat Flour
> 2 Tablespoons Oat Bran
> 2 Tablespoons Wheat Germ
> 4 Tablespoons Flax Seeds (Grind slightly)

Stir together, let stand until doubled in size, approximately 10 min:

> 1 Tablespoon sugar
> 2¼ teaspoon Yeast
> ⅓ Cup warm water

6 Tbs. cold unsalted butter cut in small pieces

2 ¼ cup ice cold water.

Add the unsalted butter into dry ingredients, mixing it on medium speed. Then add the 2¼ cup cold water to your yeast mixture, stir well and pouring slowly add it to your dry ingredients while mixer is running on medium speed. Once it forms a ball, mix for about 15 minutes longer. Dough should not be sticking to side of bowl. Should it stick, add a tablespoon of water at a time until it is not sticking. Take out dough and lightly dust with flour, return to bowl and cover with cloth or Saran wrap. Let set for 2 hours. Punch down, divide and have 2 greased bread forms ready to insert the dough. Let rise again for 45 minutes. Preheat Oven to 375° F and bake for 40 minutes. Take out of oven and turn out on rack to cool. Slice once cooled.

Submitted by Renate Hernandez. Renate is mansion web designer and photographer.

Soups

Outreach to every Man, Woman & Child!
"Welcome Home Veterans Parade" September 2018
2020 Vision Float Created to
"Celebrate 100 Years of Women's Vote."

Clam Chowder

1 dozen large clams
¼ lb. fat bacon
2 medium onions
3 medium white potatoes
Salt and pepper to taste
6 cups water
1 medium lemon

Cut bacon in small pieces and brown in bottom of kettle. Drain. Add water. Cube potatoes and onions and add to water. Simmer about 20 minutes. Add canned clams or chopped fresh clams to other ingredients. Simmer 10 minutes. Add salt and pepper to taste. Add more water if too thick. If too thin, add 2 Tbsp cornmeal. Slice lemon and add to chowder for last 5 minutes of simmering.

Submitted by: Gaynl Boma (Rhodesian Ridgebacks Champions, Companions, Therapy Dogs) in honor of Mrs. Edna Bell. In the late 1970s, I visited the Outer Banks of North Carolina. I have always loved clam chowder but this one in clear broth is my favorite. I found it in a "Roanoke Island Cookbook". The recipe is from Mrs. Edna Bell.

Slow Cooker Taco Soup

1 lb. ground beef, browned, drained
14 oz. can whole kernel corn
14 oz. can kidney beans
1 pkg. ranch dressing mix
28 oz. crushed tomatoes
14 oz. can black beans
1 pkg. taco seasoning
¼ - ½ c. chopped onion

Mix all ingredients in slow cooker and cook 6-8 hours on low.

Submitted by Hillwood FCE. In honor of Sarah Kincaid. Sarah was a member of Hillwood when Barbara Beeman joined. She said joining was the first time she defied her husband! She made arrangements for her young daughter and joined the club! She was a member until she finished her education and began teaching at Northwest High School. She always did an excellent job writing our club reports!

Cream of Celery Soup
1 cup chopped celery
1 lge. Onion, chopped
½ bay leaf
1 garlic clove, minced
2 cups water
2 Tbs. margarine
¼ cup flour
½ cup mayonnaise
½ tsp. salt
Dash of pepper
½ tsp. Worcestershire sauce
1 cup nonfat dry milk solids
Combine chopped celery, onion, bay leaf, garlic, and water. Simmer for 20 minutes. Remove bay leaf and strain. Set vegetables aside. Add water to make 2 cups liquid. Melt mayonnaise in heavy sauce pan. Stir in flour and dry milk until smooth. Slowly add reserved liquid, stirring until smooth and thickened. Add salt, pepper, and Worcestershire sauce stirring until smooth. Combine cream sauce and vegetables and process in blender until smooth. Heat and serve. Makes 4 servings.

Submitted by James Halford. In honor of his mother Margie M. Quarles.
The small bench in the kitchen of the Smith-Trahern Mansion was donated in memory of Margie by Tennessee's Western Region of which she served as President and because she loved sitting in the kitchen, usually on the steam radiator. As County President she helped with every event. She greeted cake bakers at the "Sadie Hawkins Day" Sweetheart Cake Bake dressed as Mammy Yokum and smoking a corn husk pipe.

Jeri Melton Chili Recipe
2 lbs ground beef
1 lb mild sausage
Cook on medium heat and after about 15 min add:
1 small onion chopped
Cook until meat is browned
Add 2 pkg. French's chili mix
Add 2 c water and blend all together
Add 1 large (16 - 20 oz,) can crushed tomatoes
Add 2 large or 6 small cans Bush's chili beans
Simmer for 1 hour

Another version of the chili:
1 ground turkey
1 ground chicken
1 diced bell pepper
1 c grated carrot
1 tsp ground cumin powder
1 Tbs. onion powder
1 Tbs. garlic powder
3 Tbs. chili powder or 2 more pkgs of French's chili powder
2 dashes of ground cinnamon
I large can tomato sauce
2 large or 6 small cans Bush's chili beans

Submitted by Jeri Melton. There was a place in Hillsboro Village in the past called Melton's Pharmacy. My husband Bob's parents owned and ran it. His dad was Doc Melton the pharmacist and his mom baked pies and ran the lunch counter. It was a place that was off limits for the girls from Ward Belmont because the boys hung out there. The fudge pie (see page 174) was one of the pies Mattie Ray Holder Melton cooked. Men around town still remember her pies.

Dr. Pepper Chili

1 ½ pounds ground beef
5 slices bacon
1 large onion, chopped
3-4 minced garlic cloves
2 TBSP cumin
1 TBSP oregano
3 TBSP chili powder
1-2 jalapenos, seeded and diced
Salt and pepper to taste
1 large tomato
8 oz. can tomato sauce
1 (10 ¾ oz) can tomato soup
1 can Dr. Pepper
1 tsp beef concentrate
1 block Baker's unsweetened chocolate
1 tsp cinnamon

Cook bacon crisp and set aside. Brown meat in bacon fat and set aside. Salt and pepper the meat. Add some olive oil to the pot, and when hot, add the onions and jalapenos. Cook until translucent. Add garlic and cook for 1 minute. Add the chili powder, oregano, and cumin. Cook. Add beef and bacon and cook. Add Dr. Pepper, tomato sauce, and tomato soup and bring to a simmer. Let cook 5 minutes. Add diced tomatoes and beef concentrate. Stir. Cook for 1 hour. Add chocolate and cinnamon and simmer 1 hour.

Submitted by Megan Guidry. Megan, a native Texan, came to Clarksville with her husband CPT Heath Guidry and two children as a post to Fort Campbell. A dancer, teacher, yoga, and avid reader, she volunteers her time in the community at First Christian Church, as an FRG Leader for the 1-320th FA, and children's yoga instructor at Yoga Mat. Megan looks to every moment as a way to give back to the world around her and those in it.

PICTURE THIS!

(Debby Johnson-Mansion Director, Martha M. Pile and Katie Smith)
Montgomery County Family and Community Education Organization has given their time and talents to the City-owned Christopher Smith Home. It was given the named of Smith Trahern Mansion by Martha Martin Pile in 1985 when then Mayor Ted Crozier asked her (then Extension Home Economist and Advisor to fce) if she would look into this city-owned building. The fce Organization joined in the project and have successfully maintained and improved the interior and more of this home ever since. The name honors our Lucy Smith and Margaret Trahern. Margaret spent seven years of her life restoring the home and it was in such disrepair at that time it would have been long ago torn down. This organization, in volunteer partnership with the University of Tennessee Extension, keeps the home open to the public Monday through Friday and available for others on weekends and holidays

Garlic Cheese Grits Casserole

1 cup instant "quick" grits	4 cups water
¼ pound margarine or butter	½ pound grated cheddar cheese
2 eggs – beaten	¼ cup milk
½ teaspoon garlic powder	

Preheat oven to 425 degrees. Grease a medium sized round or rectangle casserole dish. Cook the grits as directed on package with the 4 cups water. Remove from heat. Add the margarine and cheese, stirring until melted and mixed. Add the rest of ingredients and mix well. Pour into prepared casserole dish. Bake uncovered 45 to 60 minutes until bubbly and a light brown on top. Cool slightly.

Submitted by Julie Winters Reed. In honor of her mother Mary Jo Gootee Winters (12/24/1927 – 1/7/2018.) A woman who loved to celebrate, my mother made this recipe for special occasions. Even though highly educated, you could find her most days cooking for and celebrating her 14 children and beloved husband, Sam.

Wild Rice Casserole

¼ cup wild rice	¼ cup butter
3 Tbs. chopped onion	3 Tbs. chopped green pepper
3 cups hot chicken broth	

Wash rice and drain well. Melt butter in skillet. Add rice, onion, and pepper. Sautee over low heat, stirring constantly, until rice begins to turn light yellow. Turn into casserole dish and add hot chicken broth. Bake 325 degree oven for 30 minutes, until rice is tender and liquid is absorbed. Serves 4.

Submitted by James Halford. In honor of his mother Margie M. Quarles. Margie was a graduate and facilitator of Leadership Lincoln, organized a Family and Community Education Club and served as President. She became County FCE President and served as President of the Western Region FCE President. She attended several National FCE Conventions including the one to Alaska where she got to see her moose.

Cornbread Dressing

1½ skillets of cornbread made with buttermilk and cooked in Lodge cast iron

5 or 6 biscuits crumbled (biscuits purchased frozen are fine for this)

1 cup butter

1 cup very finely chopped Vidalia onions

1 stalk or so chopped celery

32 ounces of chicken broth (ideally from a hen or concentrated from chicken parts that are slow cooked with onion and celery and used for chicken salad)

1 tablespoon salt

½ teaspoon pepper

2 tablespoon sage

6 tablespoon poultry seasoning

Make cornbread and biscuits while onions and celery gently cook in the butter.

Break up the cornbread with a potato masher and mix with the biscuits.

Add most of the seasonings to the butter mixture and mix it into the crumbled bread into a very large bowl. (Hold back some of the sage and poultry seasoning if shy around flavor.)

Stir in most of the broth and make sure it looks "right." Add enough broth to make the mixture pretty wet looking, but not soupy.

Transfer into 1 or 2 large baking dishes.

Cover tightly with aluminum foil. Heat about 30 minutes at 350 degrees. If you like it browned, remove the foil toward the end.

Recipe can be doubled and the excess frozen.

Submitted by Brenda Harper. In honor of Judy Stanfill Graham. Judy Stanfill Azzara was 23 in 1972 when she defeated the incumbent, an APSU department head and her college advisor, to become the youngest office holder in Montgomery County and the youngest woman elected to a County Court in Tennessee.

Squash Dressing
3 cups cornbread crumbled
½ cup onion, chopped
½ cup celery, chopped
3 cups pureed squash
1 can each cream of celery and mushroom
1 egg
1 teaspoon parsley
2 teaspoon sage
1 cup cheese shredded
salt and black pepper to taste
Preheat oven to 350° F. Spray 9x13 casserole pan with cooking spray. Reserve ½ cup shredded cheese. Mix remaining ingredients together well. Pour into casserole pan. Bake in oven for 45 minutes. Sprinkle reserved shredded cheese on top the last five minutes. Bake until brown. Serve immediately. Serves: 6 to 8 people.

Submitted by Annette Cole. Annette is the Extension Agent in Adult and Youth Family and Consumer Science and has shared and made this recipe for many joint events at the Smith Trahern Mansion. She is recognized as a quality seamstress, known for her creativity, and was trained by well-known chef.

Smashing Squash
2 lbs of summer squash, sliced.
1 carrot pared and cut in small pieces.
1 small onion peeled and cut in small pieces.
1 stick of butter melted and mixed with 8oz of Pepperidge Farm stuffing.
Preheat oven to 350°. Cook yellow squash. Add carrot and onion and drain when tender. Salt and pepper to taste. Combine with 1 cup sour cream and 1 cup cream of chicken (or onion) soup. Top with buttered stuffing and bake 20 to 30 minutes until the top is golden brown.

Submitted by Kim McMillan. Kim was Mayor of Clarksville 2011-2018.

Squash Fritters
1 cup cooked squash, mashed and drained well
Add:

1 egg	2 Tablespoons sugar
2 Tbs. chopped onion	½ Cup self-rising flour
Salt and pepper	

Beat together and drop by tablespoons in hot Wesson Oil. Brown on both sides. Drain on paper towel.

Submitted by Judy Landiss.

Squash Casserole
2 lbs. squash, sliced
1 medium onion chopped
1 can cream of mushroom soup
1/3 cup milk
8 oz. cheddar cheese, grated
2 cups bread pieces
Butter
Salt and Pepper to taste
Cook squash and onion in small amount of water until tender: drain. Place half of this in casserole dish. Pour soup diluted with milk over squash. Sprinkle ½ cheese over squash. Sprinkle 1 cup bread pieces over squash. Sprinkle ½ cheese over bread. Add remaining squash, then remaining bread pieces, then remaining cheese. Dot with butter. Bake at 375 degrees for 25 minutes.

Submitted by Betty (Nichols) Cole. Betty is a member of Sango FCE Club and quite active in community events. As a Master Gardener, she is a dedicated member of the Montgomery County Master Gardener Association. She retired after having worked at the Montgomery County Juvenile Court for 30 years. At the 2018 Sweetheart Cake Bake, Betty won a blue ribbon for her upside-down cake.

Asparagus Casserole

1 stick butter, melted
1 large can asparagus, drained, rinsed
1½ c cracker crumbs
1 can cream of mushroom soup
½ c grated cheddar cheese
½ c broken pecans
Butter casserole dish. Mix butter and crumbs. Make layer of ½ crumbs and ½ cheese. Add asparagus and nuts. Add soup. Top with remaining cheese then crumbs. Bake at 350° for 30 minutes.

Submitted by Barbara Brown Beeman. My mother's recipe which I served to a group of college students who enjoyed it before they knew what it was. One protested, "But I hate asparagus!" Another asked me not to tell his mother that he ate asparagus! The order of preparation distinguishes this recipe from many others.

Baked Pineapple

¾ cup sugar
6 Tbs. flour
2 cups grated sharp cheese
2 cans (20 oz.) pineapple chunks drained and 6 Tbs. juice
1 cup crushed saltine crackers
8 Tbs. (1 stick) butter melted
Preheat oven to 350 degrees. Grease casserole dish.
Stir together sugar and flour. Stir in cheese. Add pineapple. Combine and pour into dish. Combine cracker crumbs, butter, and pineapple juice. Spread on top of pineapple mixture. Bake 25-30 minutes until bubbly and brown.

Submitted by Rachel Trice Johnson Pulley. Rachel was involved in FCE when she was three years old, coming to meetings with her mother. She was at a FCE County Council meeting the day we took on the mansion project.

Sweet Potato Casserole

3 cups mashed sweet potatoes	1 cup sugar
2 eggs, beaten	½ tsp. salt
½ stick butter, softened	½ cup milk
1 teaspoon vanilla	

Mix listed ingredients until well-combined and smooth.
Spread evenly in a shallow, greased casserole dish.

Combine:

1 cup brown sugar	1/3 cup flour
1/3 stick softened butter	1 cup coarsely chopped pecans

Spread across the top of the sweet potato mixture. Bake in a 350°
pre-heated oven for 35 minutes.

Submitted by Brenda Harper. In honor of Mamie Jean Hutchison
Harper. Director of the Clarksville-Montgomery County Public Library
for 25 years, Mamie Jean Harper encouraged so many Clarksvillians in
the joys of reading and life-long learning, always in a welcoming
environment.

Mariel's Sweet Potato Casserole

2 cups raw grated sweet potatoes	¾ stick of margarine melted
1¼ cup sugar	½ tsp nutmeg
2 eggs beaten	½ tsp cinnamon
1 cup of milk	

Mix all ingredients well and pour into a greased casserole dish. Bake
in 400 degree oven for 20 minutes. While this is baking, make
topping:

¾ cup crushed cornflakes	½ cup brown sugar
½ cup nuts	¾ stick melted margarine

Mix above ingredients and spread over casserole. Return to oven and
bake an additional 20 minutes.

Submitted by Mary Moore. In honor of her mother Mariel
Thompson.

Sweet Potato Pone
4 eggs
2 cups milk
1 quart grated raw potatoes
1 cup sugar
¼ cup melted butter
1 teaspoon each… nutmeg and cinnamon
½ teaspoon salt
Mix ingredients. Bake at 350 degrees until firm.

Submitted by Elizabeth W. Weaks.

Mary Jim's Cheese Soufflé
4 Tbsp butter
2 cups milk
4 Tbsp flour
2 cups grated sharp cheddar cheese
6 eggs separated
1 tsp salt
Red pepper
In heavy pan, melt butter, add flour and stir until smooth. Add milk, stir over medium heat until thick. Add beaten egg yolks, salt and red pepper and cook until the mix bubbles. Cool somewhat. Fold into beaten egg whites. Place soufflé dish in a pan of water in oven. Bake 350 degrees for about an hour. Serve immediately.

Submitted by Jim Marshall. In Honor of his mother Mary Beaumont Marshall. Mary, ninth of ten children, spent her married life on the Dunlap Lane family farm (1921-1980). She held offices for decades in the Kirkwood PTA, Home Demonstration Club, St. Bethlehem Country Woman's Club, Grace Chapel (Rossview Episcopal Ladies' Aide) and Middle Tennessee Farm Bureau Women's Association.

Kathy's Cheesy Potatoes

6 Idaho potatoes
Cheese of choice- sour cream, cream cheese, cottage cheese, etc.
2 T margarine or butter
1 T plain flour
1/2 cup milk (or half & half)
Small chopped onion
3-6 cloves of garlic peeled and finely chopped
Seasoning to taste

Peel and dice potatoes and cover in salted water in a large pot. Boil until barely done.

While potatoes are cooking, melt butter in a sauce pan.

Sauté onion until it starts to turn translucent, add chopped garlic, and cook a minute or two longer.

Stir in flour, then add milk while stirring. Remove from heat.

If using cream cheese, add it on top to soften while you work on the potatoes.

Drain potatoes. If you have cooked too soft, you may need to rinse in cool water to stop them from overcooking and turning to mush.

Add cooked onion/garlic, either sour cream or softened cream cheese until creamy looking.

Add grated cheeses of your choice.

Add seasonings of your choice.

Stir and add a little milk if it looks too dry.

You can cover and refrigerate if making the night ahead or put straight into a preheated 350° oven, uncovered.

Just cook until bubbly and top is starting to brown, about 20 minutes

Submitted by Kathy Smith, Warfield FCE.

Baked Beans
1 lb. hot Sausage
1 can (32 oz.) Pork and Beans
1 tbsp. Chili Powder
½ cup dark Karo Syrup
Cook sausage and drain well. Mix all together and bake 30 minutes at 350 degrees.

Submitted by Joy Atkins.

Pork & Beans Casserole
Sauté ½ cup onion, set aside. In a 10-inch skillet brown 1 lb. ground beef. Mix 16 ounce can of pork and beans, ½ cup Velveeta or cheddar cheese and onion into ground beef. Cut biscuit of your choice in half and place around sides of skillet. Bake 350 degrees until biscuits are brown about 15 to 20 minutes.

Submitted by Jane Bagwell. Jane is about raising the standard of living for her family and people in the community through her jobs. She worked for UT Expanded Food and Nutrition and Workforce Essentials. Her love of history is reflected in her dedication to the Stewart County Historical Society and Museum.

Jackie B's BBQ Baked Beans
1 large can Bush's baked beans
1 lb. browned ground turkey
1 med. Yellow onion (sautéed)
1 med. green Bell pepper (sautéed)
3 Tbs. Worcestershire
3 Tbs. brown sugar (more to taste)
3 Tbs. BBQ sauce
6-8 strips of bacon (optional)
Mix together all ingredients, lay bacon on top.
Bake in oven at 325 degrees for 30-45 minutes.

Submitted by Melinda Evans.

Italian Potato Casserole

1 1/3 C potato flakes
1 Tbsp reduced calorie margarine
¼ C finely chopped onion
1 clove minced garlic
½ C part-skim ricotta cheese
1 lightly beaten egg
1 oz grated parmesan cheese
2 Tbsp chopped fresh parsley
½ teaspoon salt
1/8 teaspoon pepper
2 ½ ounces shredded mozzarella cheese

In a 1-quart saucepan bring 1 ¾ C water to boil; remove from heat, add potato flakes, and stir until mixture is smooth and no lumps remain.

Preheat oven to 350 degree.

In an 8-inch skillet heat margarine over medium high heat until bubbly and hot; add onion and garlic and sauté until softened, 1 to 2 minutes.

Transfer to medium mixing bowl; add potatoes and remaining ingredients except mozzarella cheese, mixing well.

Spray 1-quart casserole with non-stick cooking spray; spread with half of the potato mixture in bottom of casserole.

Sprinkle half of the mozzarella cheese over potato mixture in casserole; top with remaining potatoes mixture then bake until top is lightly browned, 25 to 30 minutes. Makes 4 servings

Submitted by Hillwood FCE. In honor of Barbara Johnson. Barbara was a member of Hillwood FCE Club in the 1980s.

Fried Green Tomatoes

3 medium green tomatoes sliced ¼ inch thick

Salt

¼ cup cornmeal	¼ cup grated Parmesan cheese
2 Tbs. all-purpose flour	¾ tsp. dried oregano
1 egg beaten	1/8 tsp. pepper
¼ cup vegetable oil	¾ tsp. garlic salt

Lightly sprinkle tomatoes with salt. Drain on paper towels for 30-60 minutes. Meanwhile, combine cornmeal, flour, parmesan, garlic salt, oregano, and pepper in a shallow plate. Dip each tomato slice into egg and into cornmeal mixture. Fry tomatoes a few at a time, for 2 minutes per side or until golden brown. Drain on paper towels. Serve immediately.

Submitted by Frances Trice. Frances Batson Trice was born and raised in the community of Jordan Springs, which is now part of Ft. Campbell, Ky. During her marriage, she lived in Newfoundland, California, Oklahoma, and North Carolina. Although she accumulated many recipes from these different areas, she likes the southern recipes from her mother and grandmother.

Okra and Tomatoes

3 slices bacon, 2 lb. okra cut, 1 med green pepper, 1 small onion, 2 cloves garlic, 2 lb. fresh tomatoes peeled and cubed, salt and pepper to taste.

Fry bacon until crisp, drain and reserve drippings, add green pepper, onion, garlic to drippings, cook 5 minutes, stir in tomatoes, okra, add salt and pepper then bacon chipped up, put on skillet lid and cook 15 minutes.

Submitted by Linda Ellison. This recipe was given to me by my mother Mariam Haile, she always had a garden and when okra and tomatoes were in season. This dish was the family favorite.

Poke Pie
Pick about a plastic grocery bag of poke. After washing, boil until tender, drain well, and chop. Brown 4 or 5 strips of bacon. Mix reserved grease with poke, crumbled bacon, ¾ cup cheese and 3 to 4 eggs depending on size. Pour mix into unbaked pie shell and bake at 350 degrees for about 45 minutes until pie is set and crust is brown.

Submitted by Jane Bagwell. In honor of her grandmother Rosabell Heflin born 1891. What I remember about my grandmother is every morning, after breakfast she would go out and milk cows. She would bring in the milk and churn butter. She made the best buttermilk I ever tasted in my life.

Gnocchi

6 cups flour	3 pounds ricotta cheese
3 eggs	1/8 teaspoon salt

Mix ricotta, eggs and salt in large bowl. Add 5 cups flour, mix well. Knead until dough is formed adding remaining flour gradually, until not too soft. Pinch a piece at a time and roll forming a finger like roll. Cut into 1-inch lengths. Press each piece with the thumb against the concave surface of a cheese grater, to give the appearance of a shell. Place on floured surface. Bring a pot of salted water to a boil and drop in gnocchi. Reduce heat to medium. They will rise to the top. Cook 12 to 15 minutes. Drain and serve with spaghetti sauce.

Submitted by Hillwood FCE. In honor of Doris Haywood (Via Elmo Cheachi.) Doris moved to Clarksville from Indiana and was a former member of Hillwood FCE Club.

Vicki Allen's Broccoli Recipe
Cup mayo, 2 cans cream of chicken, 1 cup- shredded cheddar cheese, stir it up. Cook Broccoli and stir in. Put in baking dish, bake at 375° 30-45 minutes. Take butter crackers and crumble on top if you want.

Submitted by Vicki Allen.

Meats & Main Dishes

2020 Vision Committee – Created to Celebrate the 100th Anniversary of Suffrage, an on-going effort since 2015.

Chicken and Dumplings

Stew the chicken until done, remove from broth, debone and skin, cut in pieces and place back in broth. Next make dumplings, 2 cups flour, 2 whole eggs, beaten, ¼ tsp. soda, 6 tbs. shortening, ½ tsp. salt, 1/8 tsp. baking powder. Mix flour, soda, salt and baking powder. Cut with shortening, then add enough liquid, either water or broth with eggs pour into dry mixture, making stiff dough roll out thin, cut into small pieces, drop into boiling broth of stewed chicken turn low heat, cover, let set and cool for a few minutes until done.

Submitted by Linda Ellison. In honor of her grandmother, Clara Logan Disney. My grandmother was a true mountain woman, raising her garden, canning food, and sewing for her children. She was also a charter member of the Kentucky homemakers (FCE) club in Knox County Ky. I remember seeing her wring the chicken by the neck to make this dish.

Chicken Enchiladas

1 pint sour cream
2 cans cream of chicken soup
1 (about 7 ounce) can of diced green chilies
1 lb. sharp cheddar shredded + ½ lb. Monterey Jack mixed together
Shredded chicken (2-3 cooked boneless, skinless chicken breasts)
12-14 soft taco size tortillas
Mix sour cream, soup, and chilies in a sauce pan and heat. Put cooked chicken, cheese and a spoonful of soup mixture in each tortilla. Roll and place in 9x13 baking dish. Cover with remaining soup mixture and cheese. Bake at 350° for 25 minutes until cheese is bubbly. If it has been refrigerated, add 10-20 minutes to cook time.

Submitted by: Annie Albaro in honor of her grandmother Mary Gable. I got the chance to visit my grandmother while we were in Arizona for a FCE conference a couple years ago and this is what she made for dinner. Before we left she gave me this recipe and it has become a family favorite.

Chicken Enchilada Penne Pasta

1 (16 oz.) pkg. penne pasta
2 Tbs. olive oil
1 onion, diced
1 red bell pepper, diced
2 cloves garlic, minced
2 cooked chicken breasts, shredded (or more to taste)
2 10 oz. cans green enchilada sauce
2/3 cup red enchilada sauce
1 4 oz. can diced green chilies
2 tsp. chili powder
1 tsp. ground cumin
½ tsp. salt
2 cups shredded Colby-Monterey Jack cheese
1 cup sour cream

Bring a large pot of lightly salted water to a boil; add penne and cook, stirring occasionally, until tender, yet firm, about 11 minutes. Drain and return pasta to pot. Heat oil in a large deep skillet over medium high heat. Sauté onion in hot oil until slightly softened, 3-5 minutes. Stir in red bell pepper and garlic, sauté until fragrant and softened, 3-5 minutes. Stir chicken, enchilada sauces, diced green chilies, and seasonings into onion mixture. Reduce heat to low and simmer until flavors blend, 8 to 10 minutes. Add cheese, stir until melted and heated through, 1-3 minutes. Stir sour cream into enchilada mixture and stir until heated through. Pour enchilada mixture over penne pasta and toss to coat completely.

Submitted by Lindsey White. Lindsey has worked in Greece & Nigeria for the State Department and is most dedicated to her son Rhys.

Chicken with Olive Rice

1 (3 ½ pound) frying chicken
Milk
¼ pound butter
½ cup sifted all-purpose flour
1 tsp salt
1 tsp paprika
Dash cayenne
1 ½ cups brown rice
1 cup ripe olives
3 cups chicken broth (or 4 chicken bouillon cubes dissolved in water)
Salt and pepper
½ tsp powdered thyme
1 (4 oz.) can mushrooms and liquid

Have chicken cut into serving pieces. Dip in milk then in flour which has been blended with salt, paprika, thyme and cayenne. Melt butter in shallow baking pan (9X13X2") Place chicken skin side down in butter. Bake 400 degrees about 30 minutes. Turn chicken pieces over and bake about 20 minutes longer. Meanwhile cut olives in large pieces, reduce heat to 350. Remove chicken from pan and stir unwashed rice into butter. Add broth and undrained mushrooms and boil about 5 minutes. Season to taste with salt and pepper. Add olives. Turn into large casserole dish and place chicken pieces on top. Cover and bake 1 hour longer or until chicken and rice are tender and liquid absorbed. Makes about 5 servings.

Submitted by Andrea Zavatchen. In honor of her mother Margery Ellen Evans. Margery Ellen Evans was English and an excellent cook. She lived in England, Germany, Hawaii, and three other states. She collected recipes everywhere she lived, and she found this recipe while living in Hawaii.

Crock Pot Chicken
Chicken
Tomatoes
Cilantro
Lime juice
Chili powder or taco seasoning
Put in layers as listed. Turn on high for 6 to 8 hours, turn to low for longer.

Submitted by Debby Johnson. December 2009, Debby was named 2nd Director of the Smith Trahern Mansion. 2014 on County "2020 Vision" committee, 2018 DAR, Capt. William Edmiston Chapter. Member of Sunnyview Homemakers club since 1980 and Sango FCE since 2003. In 2018 Debby became seamstress for the APSU Governors football team, repairing jerseys.

Filipino Chicken or Pork Adobo

2 lbs. chicken (or pork)
6 cloves garlic minced
½ teaspoon black pepper
½ teaspoon of Accent (optional)
2 tablespoons vegetable oil
2 big potatoes, cubed

½ cup white vinegar
1 white/yellow onion chopped
¾ cup Kikoman soy sauce
5 cups water (or chicken stock)
1-2 pieces of bay leaves
Pinch of sugar

Boiled whole eggs (optional) 5-6 hard boiled
In non-stick medium pot, sauté onions in vegetable oil until translucent. Add garlic and cook a minute more. Place meat in pot &brown. Add 5 cups of stock or water, vinegar, bay leaves, pepper, sugar, and soy sauce. Stir and cover. Simmer chicken for about 40-45 minutes until meat is tender. Pork takes longer to tenderize (90 mins.) Add potatoes when meat is almost tender. Boiled eggs are optional. Enjoy! Serve over white rice. Serves 8.

Submitted by Susan White.

Simple Chicken and Sausage Gumbo

1 cup oil

1 cup flour

2 large onions chopped

2 bell peppers chopped

4 ribs celery chopped

4 - 6 cloves garlic, minced

4 quarts chicken stock

2 bay leaves

2 teaspoons Creole seasoning, or to taste

1 teaspoon dried thyme leaves

Salt and freshly ground black pepper to taste

1 large chicken (young hen preferred), cut into pieces

2 pounds Andouille/smoked sausage/kielbasa cut into 1/2" pieces

1 bunch scallions (green onions), tops only, chopped

2/3 cup fresh chopped parsley

Filé powder to taste

Season the chicken with salt, pepper and Creole seasoning and brown quickly. Brown the sausage, pour off fat and reserve meats.

In a large, heavy pot, heat the oil and cook the flour in the oil over medium to high heat (depending on your roux-making skill), stirring constantly, until the roux reaches a dark reddish-brown color, almost the color of coffee or milk chocolate for a Cajun-style roux. If you want to save time, or prefer a more New Orleans-style roux, cook it to a medium, peanut-butter color, over lower heat if you're nervous about burning it. Add the vegetables and stir quickly. This cooks the vegetables and also stops the roux from cooking further. Continue to cook, stirring constantly, for about 4 minutes. Add the stock, seasonings, chicken and sausage. Bring to a boil, cook for about one hour, skimming fat off the top as needed. Add the chopped scallion tops and parsley, and heat for 5 minutes. Serve over rice in large shallow bowls. Accompany with lots of hot, crispy French bread.

YIELD: About 12 entrée sized servings.

Submitted by Martha Pile.

Carolina Pork BBQ
5-6 pounds fresh pork shoulder
Salt, pepper, garlic
1 tbs. Liquid smoke
Place pork into crock pot season and cook on low over night until tender and pulls apart easily. (About 8 hours). Discard liquid and fat. Shred and return to crock pot.
Sauce:
½ Cup margarine
1 Cup vinegar
½ Cup catsup/ketchup
Couple dashes of hot sauce
2 Bay leaves
2 medium onions finely chopped
½ Cup brown sugar
1 clove of garlic pressed or minced
1 Tbs. dry mustard
¼ tsp. cayenne pepper
1 tsp. black pepper
1 tsp. salt
Mix all ingredients in a sauce pan and bring to a boil. Reduce heat and simmer uncovered for 30 minutes. Remove bay leaves. Pour sauce over shredded pork in the crock pot. Cook on low for another 4-8 hours. The longer it cooks, the sweeter it gets. Serve with buns and coleslaw.

Submitted by: Sandra Brennan.

Barbecued Pork on Bun
1 cup diced leftover pork
2 Tbs. brown sugar
1 Tbs. Worcestershire sauce
½ cup ketchup
2 Tbs. vinegar
Heat together and serve on buns.

Submitted by Doris Fairrow.

Beef Medallions

1 pound beef sliced into 1 inch pieces	4 sliced mushrooms
1 clove of garlic sliced finely	½ cup heavy cream
1/2 stick of butter	garlic salt
Rice servings for two	1 cup Marsala wine

Cook the rice with a small amount of salt. Beat out the beef with tenderizing mallet to add more tenderness. Cook the beef in a large skillet with the garlic and mushrooms in butter until beef is well browned. Add garlic salt to taste. When nearing completion, turn the heat to high. As the meat, garlic, and mushrooms begin to sizzle, turn off the heat and add the wine. Set the mixture on fire with a lighter. It will burn for about 15 seconds. The moment it goes out, pour in the heavy cream and stir. Pour the mixture over the rice and add a side or baguette with some brie for a delicious meal.

Submitted by Jim Smith. Jim is a member of Warfield FCE and lives in downtown Guthrie, KY. He is a man of faith and enjoys music and writing songs.

"Chicken" Enchilada Casserole

1-pound ground meat	1 small onion (chopped)
1 can cream of chicken soup	13 ounce can of evaporated milk
7 ounce can of diced green chilies	1 small can enchilada sauce
1 pkg. of tortillas (cut into quarters)	½ to ¾ cup of cheddar cheese

Fry ground beef and onion until brown. Add can of cream of chicken soup, chilies, and enchilada sauce. Preheat oven at 350°. Grease casserole dish, pour mixture to cover the bottom. Place tortillas (or can substitute Fritos) on top. Repeat, finishing with the soup mixture. Top with cheddar cheese. Bake for 30-40 minutes.

Submitted by Pamela McIntyre Albaro. I am the third generation to make this recipe for my family. My grandmother (father's side) and mother would make several of these and freeze them, so we could eat them later. My children laugh at the name and lack of "chicken" in the casserole.

Standing Rib Roast with Aioli
1-shoulder-and-4-bone standing beef rib-eye roast, preferably dry-aged (around 8 pounds) chine bone removed.
Kosher salt
freshly ground pepper
2 large egg yolks
2 cloves garlic, finely grated
½ cup grape-seed or vegetable oil
1 tablespoon fresh lemon juice
½ cup extra virgin olive oil
Generously season beef with salt and pepper. Wrap tightly in plastic and chill at least 1 day.
Let beef sit at room temperature for 2 hours.
Preheat oven to 400 degrees.
Place beef on rack set inside a roasting pan. Roast until nicely browned 35-40 minutes. Reduce oven temperature to 275 degrees and continue roasting until an instant read thermometer inserted into the thickest part of beef reads 115 degrees; for medium rare, 1-1 ½ hours longer
Transfer roast onto a cutting board with ribs pointed upward and let rest at least 30 minutes.
Meanwhile, whisk egg yolks and garlic in medium bowl. Whisking constantly, gradually add grape-seed oil drop-by-drop at first, and whisk, adding 1 tablespoon of lemon juice by the teaspoonful as aioli thickens (juice will thin aioli so it is easier to whisk,) until it is thicken and smooth. Gradually whisk in olive oil, adding water by the teaspoonful if it gets too thick. Season with salt; cover and chill.
Cut meat off bones following curve of the ribs and thinly slice, or cut between ribs for massive chops for sharing. Serve with aioli.

Submitted by Carol Stichal. I moved to Clarksville in 2001 and was placed at the mansion through the National Council on Aging training program. I joined Belmont FCE where I served as club president and later county council president. In 2015, I moved back to California.

Lasagna

¾ lb ground beef	1 Tsp parsley
¾ lb. ground pork	1 Tsp basil
1 onion	1 Tsp Oregano
Can of crushed tomatoes	Lasagna noodles
Can of tomato puree	salt/pepper
15 oz of Riccota cheese	parmesan cheese
2 large packages Mozzarella cheese	1 egg

Brown meat with chopped onion, salt, parsley, basil and oregano. Add crushed tomatoes and tomato puree. Make sure it is rich with tomato. Add another can of puree if needed. Simmer. Cook lasagna noodles until they are not quite tender. Mix ricotta cheese with one egg and pepper. Layer in pan: meat sauce, noodles, then spread ricotta cheese on noodles, sprinkle parmesan cheese then a layer of mozzarella cheese. Repeat. Finish with noodles, mozzarella and meat sauce. Bake at 350 degrees for about 30 minutes.

Submitted by: Shirley Griffy Winn. Shirley taught elementary school for 33 years and joined Sango FCE after retirement. She played golf, mentored student teachers, and volunteered at local schools in addition to FCE activities.

Scalloped Oyster Casserole

2 cans (for small dish) 4 cans (for large) Bull Head canned oysters

Saltines	Milk
Pepper to taste	Butter

Oil deep casserole dish. Crumble crackers into layer in dish only ½". Dot crackers with butter. Layer oysters over crackers. Moisten with milk and juice from oysters. Pepper to taste. Repeat layers until you use all the oysters. Put final layer of crackers on top. Dot with butter and moisten the casserole with milk mixture, until fairly juicy, but not watery. Bake 350 for 45-50 minutes, until very "bubbly."

Submitted by Chris Crow. In honor of his mother Lillie Bell Hunter Crow (1917-2004).

Shrimp Recipe

To two cups very thick white sauce, add two egg yolks just as sauce is ready to be taken from heat. Melt ½ lb butter, stir in ¾ cup lemon juice. Add to sauce. Then add:

1 cup mushrooms, chopped	3 cups celery, diced
2 cups truffles mushrooms, diced	6 cups (2 lbs) cooked shrimp
Salt to taste	

Let stand in refrigerator at least 12 hours. Reheat over boiling water. Serves 12.

Submitted by Rubye Patch. In honor of Margaret Fort Trahern (1902-1966). Margaret Dancy Fort had played as a child in the yard of the antebellum Christopher Smith home. In 1947, Margaret's husband, Joseph purchased the home, which was then in sad disrepair. Together, they restored it to its former glory. APSU English teacher and art patron, Margaret offered the home with its great halls, upstairs and down, to college students for their social functions. The first fine arts building on campus bears her name.

Salmon Croquettes

½ stick butter	1 16 oz. can of salmon
¼ cup flour	1 small onion chopped
½ tsp. salt	2 tbs. green peas
½ cup evaporated milk	1 tsp. chopped pimento
Cracker crumbs	

Melt butter in sauce pan. Add flour, salt, and milk. Cook over medium heat until sauce is thick. Add remaining ingredients. Shape into croquettes, roll in fine cracker crumbs, slightly beaten egg, and then again in cracker crumbs. Fry in shallow fat, turning when necessary to brown nicely.

Submitted by Katie Smith. In honor of her grandmother Kate Dortch Fitch. Kate was born in 1894, one of the youngest in a large farm family. She said when she was 8 years old, her job was to make "biscuit" for breakfast and sweep the floor every day.

Salmon Quiche

1 cup whole wheat Flour	2/3 cup shredded sharp cheddar cheese
¼ cup chopped almonds	½ teaspoon salt
¼ teaspoon paprika	6 tablespoons oil
1 large can salmon	3 beaten eggs
1 cup sour cream	¼ cup salad dressing
1 tablespoon grated onion	¼ tsp. dried dill weed
½ cup shredded cheese	3 drops hot pepper sauce

Crust: flour, cheese, almond, salt, paprika, stir in oil. Set aside ½ cup of this mixture. Press remaining into greased pie pan. Bake at 400 degrees for 10 minutes. Drain Salmon and reserve liquid. Add water to liquid to make ½ cup. Blend together eggs, sour cream, mayo and liquid. Stir in salmon, ½ cup cheese, dillweed, and hot pepper sauce. Spoon into crust; sprinkle with reserve crust mix. Bake at 325 for 45 minutes.

Submitted by Hillwood FCE. In honor of Peggy Roddy. Peggy was Hillwood President, Montgomery County Council President, and participant of the 75th Anniversary of the Women's Right to Vote.

Lazy Man Pierogis

1 small can mushrooms drained	1 16 oz. can of sauerkraut
1 onion diced	1 lb. fatty bacon diced
1 can cream of mushroom soup	1 lb. small spiral pasta shell

Fry bacon with onion. Drain. Cook sauerkraut 5 minutes. Drain. Add mushrooms and sauerkraut to bacon and onion mixture. Fry 10 minutes. Cook spirals until almost done. Drain. Add mushroom soup to frying pan mixture and pour over spirals.

Submitted by Andrea Zavatchen. I first joined a Homemaker's Club in the 1970s, but dropped out when I went to work full time in 1999. I worked for the Montgomery County School System and Phila Hach before going to work for the State of Tennessee. I returned to FCE after retirement in 2017.

Bluff House Simple Shrimp and Grits
1 (14.5 oz.) can reduced-sodium chicken broth
4 tablespoons unsalted butter, divided
6 tablespoons quick-cooking grits
3 tablespoons sharp white cheddar cheese, cut into small chunks
5 ounces evaporated milk or half-and-half
½ cup chopped scallions, white and green parts
½ pound uncooked medium shrimp, peeled and deveined*
3 tablespoons fresh lemon juice
Combine chicken broth and 1 tablespoon butter in a heavy, medium-sized saucepan. Bring to a boil.
Slowly stir in grits, keeping smooth. Reduce heat to low and simmer 5 minutes, stirring occasionally.
Mix cheese and milk into grits, stirring frequently, until creamy, about 4 minutes.
Melt remaining 3 tablespoons butter in a heavy skillet over medium high heat. Add shrimp and sauté just until shrimp are pink and cooked through, 2 or 3 minutes. Stir in lemon juice and simmer about 2 minutes.
Spoon grits into center of a heated plate. Top with shrimp, drizzle with lemon butter from skillet, sprinkle with scallions. Serves 2.
*I only make this with wild-caught, shells-on Gulf shrimp.

Submitted by Sharon Crisp. In honor of Dee W. Boaz. Dee was editor of The Leaf-Chronicle newspaper in Clarksville, TN during 1983-1994. She was co-founder of Leadership Clarksville, the Museum's Flying High fundraiser, and The Network (a women's leadership group). Dee served on and/or led state and national newspaper boards.

Cakes

Smith Trahern Mansion "Home of Family and Community Education" (101 McClure St.) is owned by the city and is operated & staffed daily by fce volunteers. The annual Sweetheart Cake Bake fund raiser goes to the upkeep of the interior and meet other needs of the antebellum home. The flower gardens are projects of the Master Gardeners. **Educational Programs** include the dissemination of research-based information/best practices in Family and Consumer Science from the University of Tennessee & Tennessee State University. Pictured are some of Sango fce Members and Mansion Volunteers (L to R) Seated-Shirley Winn, Katie Smith, Pat Woods; standing - Martha Pile, Debby Johnson (Mansion Director), Andrea Zavatchen & Brenda Harper.

Yellow Cake with Caramel Icing
Cake:
2 ¼ Cups sifted cake flour
3 ½ teaspoons baking powder
1 tsp. salt
1 2/3 cups sugar
2/3 cup Crisco
1 ¾ cups milk
3 eggs
1 tsp. vanilla
Measure dry ingredients and Crisco into mixing bowl. Blend thoroughly by hand or mixer at medium speed for 2 minutes. Add milk, eggs, and vanilla and mix on medium speed for 2 more minutes. Pour into greased 9 x 11 cake pan. Bake 350-degree oven for about 35 minutes.

Caramel Icing:
2 ½ cups sugar
½ cup boiling water
1 stick butter
1 cup evaporated milk
1 Tbs. Crisco
¾ tsp. salt
To caramelize sugar, add ½ cup sugar into skillet. Brown as you desire then add ½ cup boiling water and caramelize. Add remaining sugar, milk, butter, salt, and Crisco into saucepan and bring to a boil. Add caramelized sugar syrup. Cook until forms a soft ball when dropped in cold water. Remove from stove, add vanilla, and beat until it reaches spreading consistency.

Submitted by Delinia Storr. In honor of Alberta Ogburn. Alberta was a woman of elegance and grace, humble and strong in Christian faith. She was a supporter, participant, and leader in FCE for many years. She was the president of Warfield club and Warfield became one of the first clubs to meet at night so that more women could participate.

White Cake with Caramel Icing
Cake:
2 1/3 cup sifted cake flour
¾ cup shortening
1 cup buttermilk
½ tsp. baking soda
1 tsp. baking powder
1 tsp. vanilla
1 tsp. salt
1 2/3 cup sugar
3 eggs
Sift flour, baking powder, soda, salt and sugar together. Place shortening, buttermilk and flavoring in a large bowl. Add sifted dry ingredients and blend.
Beat 2 minutes (med speed) add eggs and beat 1 more minute. Bake 350° for 35 minutes. Makes 2 nice high layers, 9-inch layers.

Caramel Icing: 3 cups sugar, 2 sticks butter; brown lightly in large pan; when begins to turn brown add 1 ½ cup evaporated milk (1 large can) cook until soft boil stage, remove from heat add ½ tsp. vanilla flavoring beat a little, spread on cake.

Submitted by Bona Perry. Bona is creative and generous. She served as the first FCE president and was chairman of the first Sweetheart Cake bake fundraiser. As an active community leader, she was an avid conservationist on her farm and in her home.

Coconut Cake
1 pkg. Duncan Hines Yellow Cake Mix
4 eggs
1 pkg. Jell-O instant pudding
½ cup Mazola oil
1 cup water
Bake at 375 degrees in two 9 inch pans
Slice each layer and put the following between each layer:
6 oz. can coconut
1½ cups sugar
1 carton sour cream
1 small can crushed pineapple (drained)
Icing:
Place in double boiler:
2 egg whites
¾ cup sugar
1/3 cup white corn syrup
1/3 cup water
Dash of cream of tartar
½ tsp. salt
1½ tsp. vanilla
1½ tsp lemon flavoring
Combine all ingredients except flavorings in top of double boiler.
Beat with electric mixer at low speed for 30 seconds, then set pan
over boiling water. Beating at high speed, cook the frosting until it is
stiff and glossy. Remove from heat and add flavorings. Beat an
additional 2 minutes. Frost sides and top of cake.

Submitted by Andrea Zavatchen. In memory of Willie Ruth
Zavatchen. My mother-in-law, Ruth Zavatchen, was born in
Tennessee and a good traditional southern cook. Like all of us, she
made mistakes and the family all remembers the year she mistakenly
added cornmeal instead of flour to the boiled custard.

Coconut Cake

1 box yellow cake mix	1 can Eagle brand milk
1 can cream of coconut mix	10 oz. container Cool Whip
Angel flake coconut	

Prepare yellow cake in oblong pan according to package directions. Combine Eagle Brand milk and Cream of Coconut mix and pour over cake which has holes in the top. Allow cake to cool; then top with cool whip and coconut. Refrigerate.

Submitted by Hillwood FCE. In honor of Nancy Neal. Nancy joined Hillwood just after it was chartered and until her health declined, she made a point not to miss meetings. She served as club President, County Council President, Regional officer, State Vice President of Programs, and on National Boards and attended many NAFCE Conferences. She served as the Books for Newborns chairperson for many years and was a graduate of original FCE institute. She also created the first public garden at Riverside Drive. She passed away Wednesday September 19, 2018. She will be greatly missed by the members of Montgomery County FCE.

Coconut Cake

1 Box Duncan Hines yellow Butter Cake Mix baked as directed on box. **Icing:** Combine 1 box powdered sugar, 8 oz. sour cream, 12 oz. frozen coconut. Divide cake into 4 equal parts with cut side up. Ice each layer and stack. Sides of cake will not be iced. Refrigerate- Better second and third day.

Submitted by Ruth Fitzgerald. Ruth is a member of Belmont FCE club where she served as club president while she was serving as County President. She accepted the opportunity to join the Extension agent in creating a home for the organization by restoring and managing the Smith Trahern Mansion. She graciously accepted a newly created position as mansion director. She served in the volunteer capacity for 25 years. The front drive was in recognition of her years of service by the city of Clarksville mayor Johnny Piper.

Amazing German Chocolate Cake

1 package plain German chocolate cake mix   1 cup water
1/3 cup vegetable oil   3 large eggs
1 container (15 ounces) coconut pecan frosting

Preheat oven to 350°. Lightly mist a 12-cup Bundt pan with vegetable oil spray, then dust with flour. Set pan aside. Place the cake mix, frosting, water, oil and eggs in a large mixing bowl. Blend with an electric mixer on low speed for 1 minute. Increase mixture speed to medium and beat 2 more minutes. Scrape sides down again if needed. Pour the batter into the pan. Bake 48 to 52 minutes.

Submitted by Nancye Britton.

Chocolate Pound Cake

3 sticks of butter   3 cups flour
3 cups sugar   2/3 cup cocoa
5 eggs   ½ tsp. baking powder
1 cup milk   2 tsp. vanilla

Soften butter to room temperature and then mix together with sugar until well blended. Add 1 egg at a time, blending well. Mix together flour, cocoa, and baking powder in a separate bowl. Mix together milk and vanilla in a measuring cup. Alternately add the flour mixture and the milk mixture to the egg and sugar mixture. When well blended, bake in a 400 degree oven until a toothpick comes out clean. The time will vary depending on the pan used. You may use several loaf pans (if making for gifts) or a Bundt cake pan.

Submitted by Anne Davis, former First Lady of Nashville. One hundred years ago, my grandmother Frances Bond was a young woman marching through the streets of Nashville to give women the right to vote. Days later, the 19th Amendment was passed, and Frances voted in every election that was held over the next 80 years. She saw her voting power as a privilege, not a chore.

Chocolate Pound Cake

3 C cake flour	½ teaspoon baking powder
¼ teaspoon salt	¼ C cocoa
½ pound margarine	3 C sugar
5 eggs	1 C milk
1 teaspoon vanilla	½ C vegetable oil

Mix margarine, sugar and oil in mixer. Add eggs one at a time. Sift Dry ingredients together. Add to margarine, sugar mixture. Add 1 cup milk and vanilla as you mix. Bake in preheated oven at 325° for one hour.

Frosting

3 C powdered sugar	3 Tbsp cocoa
2/3 C milk	¾ C butter
1Tbsp vanilla	

Mix powder sugar and cocoa in the mixer. Scald milk add butter and vanilla. Add the milk mixture to the sugar mixture, a little at the time, until it spreads like butter. Frost while hot.

Submitted by: Hillwood Club. In honor of Flora Richbourg. Flora was a retired Principal who joined Hillwood FCE.

Chocolate Sheath Cake

Sift together in mixing bowl and set aside 2 c. sugar and 2 c. flour. Bring to rolling boil: 1 stick butter, 4 t. cocoa, 1 c. water, and 1/2 c. shortening. Remove from heat and add to sugar and flour. Mix well and add: 2 eggs, slightly beaten, 1/2 c. buttermilk, 1 t. soda, 1 t. cinnamon, and 1 t. vanilla. Pour into large greased pan 16" x 11" and bake 20-25 minutes at 400. Pour over cake right out of the oven.
Icing: Bring to boil in pan: 1 stick butter, 6 T milk, and 4 T cocoa. Remove from heat and add: 1 box powdered sugar and 1 t. vanilla. Beat well until smooth and add 1 c. chopped nuts, if desired. Spread over hot cake.

Submitted by: Hillwood Club. In honor of Cathy Thomas, an early, very artistic member of Hillwood FCE.

Swiss Chocolate Cake

1 Box Swiss Chocolate cake mix	1 cup oil
1 Small box vanilla instant pudding	1 ½ cups buttermilk

Combine all ingredients. Pour into 3 round 9 inch cake pans. Bake at 350 degrees for 25 to 30 minutes.

Frosting:

8 oz. package cream cheese (softened)	16 oz. Cool-Whip
½ cup sugar	2 Hershey bars, grated
1 cup powdered sugar	

Combine and mix all but a small amount of candy for garnish. Spread frosting between layers. Garnish with remaining candy. Refrigerate.

Submitted by Jane Morrison.

Mississippi Mud Cake

2 sticks butter, melted	1/3 cup cocoa
2 cup sugar	1 ½ cup self-rising flour
4 eggs	1 cup chopped nuts
1 tsp. vanilla	10 oz. bag miniature marshmallows

Prepare 13 x 9 inch pan. Mix butter, sugar, and eggs. Add cocoa, flour, nuts, and vanilla. Bake 350 degrees 25-35 minutes. Spread marshmallows over hot cake.

Icing:

½ cup butter	1 box Confectioner's sugar
½ cup cocoa	1 tsp. vanilla
1/3 cup buttermilk	

Heat together butter, cocoa and buttermilk. Stir in confectioner's sugar and vanilla. Pour hot frosting over marshmallows and hot cake.

Submitted by Katie Smith. In honor of her mother Mary Murrell Fitch. Mary got her master's degree in Chemistry. She said when she married, her only housekeeping skill was setting a proper table. As her daughter, I have always "set a proper table."

Easy Breezy Chocolate Bundt Cake
1 box chocolate cake mix
1 small box instant chocolate pudding
8 oz. sour cream
3 eggs
¾ cup oil
¾ cup water
1 t. vanilla
8 oz. chocolate chips
Preheat oven to 350 degrees. Mix all ingredients together, except for chocolate chips, in a mixing bowl until smooth and creamy. Add in the chocolate chips. Pour into greased Bundt pan. Bake 50-60 minutes on middle rack. If you want to, you can serve it with heated chocolate sauce or sprinkle a little powdered sugar on it for looks.

Quick Fudge Frosting:
3 ¾ cups Confectioner's Sugar
½ cup cocoa powder
¼ teaspoon salt
6 Tablespoons boiling water
1 teaspoon vanilla
½ cup butter or margarine
Combine sugar, cocoa, salt, with mixer beat in boiling water, vanilla and butter until smooth. If frosting Bundt cake, you can use ½ recipe.

Submitted by Cindy Pitts. Cindy is a published author who is known for her gracious presentations. She is devoted to her family and is the wife of Clarksville's newly elected Mayor Joe Pitts.

Ella Donley's 22-Minute Chocolate Cake

2 cups sugar
2 cups flour
2 sticks margarine
3 ½ tablespoons cocoa
1 cup water
½ cup buttermilk
2 eggs
1 teaspoon soda
1 teaspoon vanilla
Icing ingredients:
3 ½ tablespoons cocoa
1/3 cup buttermilk
1 stick margarine
1 box powdered sugar

Put sugar and flour into a large bowl and set aside.
Combine margarine, cocoa, and water in a saucepan. Bring to a boil. Then mix with flour and sugar.
Beat together buttermilk, eggs, soda, and vanilla. Stir into above mixture.
Pour into a greased 9"x13"x2" pan. Bake at 325 degrees for about 20 minutes or until a toothpick comes out clean.

Icing:
Combine all icing ingredients in a saucepan and bring to a boil. Remove from heat. Add powdered sugar. Ice cake while it is still warm.
Tip: Buttermilk can be simulated by adding lemon juice or cider vinegar to regular milk.

Submitted by Ellen Kanervo. Mrs. Donley, our daughter's babysitter and substitute grandmother for eight years, did not drive. Every Election Day she asked us to drop her at her polling place so she could vote.

Pioneer Wedding Cake
1 cup brown sugar
1 cup buttermilk
¼ cup butter
6 cups plain flour
2 tsp ginger
4 tsp soda
1 tsp salt
3 whole eggs
2 tsp lemon flavoring or vanilla
1 cup molasses
Cream butter and sugar; add eggs and beat by hand. Add lemon, molasses, and buttermilk. Sift flour, soda, salt, and ginger together. Add flour mixture to other ingredients slowly (a little at a time). Beat well after each addition. Mixture will be stiff enough to roll out on a dough board. Knead dough, roll out to 1/8" thick, and cut into circles of 8" or 9" plate. Bake in prepared pan at 425 degrees until brown. Stack layers together with apple butter, applesauce, or home jam (your favorite) between each layer.
Repeat this recipe until you have 4 stacks of 6 layers, a total of 24. DO NOT stack all 24 together or it may fall over. If you do not wish to cut layers before baking, don't roll out, instead fill pan about ½ to ¾ full, making sure each layer is equal for stacking ease.
(Spice cake mix will also work for this, just add flavoring and let the layers cool before assembling in each stack)

Submitted by Anita Ellison. In honor of Mrs. Webb. Mrs. Webb lived to be 90+ and her mother often made this cake, but perhaps not all the layers. Her daughters put this in the old church cookbook. Mrs. Gunter, Mrs. Webb's mom, had about 14 children and often used "hickory" nuts in her baking as they lived on a large, old time farm. My mom said everyone loved Mrs. Gunter's cakes. People often called it a molasses or 'Lasses cake.

Four Layer Carrot Cake

1 cup canola oil	2 cups all-purpose flour
½ cup melted butter	2 tsp. baking soda
2 cups sugar	1 tsp salt
4 large eggs	2 tsp. ground cinnamon
4 cups grated carrots	1 tsp. nutmeg

1 /2 cup chopped Georgia pecans

In the bowl of an electric mixer, beat oil, melted butter, and sugar. Add eggs to mixture one at a time. In a large bowl, stir together all dry ingredients and add to sugar mixture, a little at a time until blended. Fold in carrots and pecans.

Line bottoms of two 9" round cake pans with wax paper. Evenly divide batter between pans and bake at 300 degrees for 40-50 minutes in a pre-heated oven on the middle rack. Cool the pans on wire racks for 10 minutes. Run a plastic knife around the edge of each layer and invert each onto a rack, then invert them again onto another rack so the cakes are right side up. Allow to cool completely. Make the cake layers ahead and freeze them separately wrapped in waxed paper. This makes cutting them into 4 layers and frosting easier. I use a large serrated knife.

Cream Cheese Icing for Layers:

1 pound powdered confectioners' sugar	½ stick butter, softened
8 oz. cream cheese, softened	2 tsp. vanilla extract

Beat all together with mixer until smooth. Frost between layers.

Butter Cream Icing for Top and Sides:

1 stick butter at room temperature	3-4 Tbs. whole milk
1 pound confectioner's sugar	2 tsp. vanilla extract

Beat all together with electric mixer until smooth and spreading consistency. Use to ice top and side of cake. Decorate top of cake with ¾ cup of finely chopped roasted pecans.

Submitted by Karen Edmundson. Karen was a winner of the Smith Trahern Cake Bake with this recipe!

Old Fashion Orange Cake

2 cups sugar	1 cup margarine
4 eggs	1 ¼ cups milk + 1 tsp of baking soda
4 cups all-purpose flour	1 cup chopped pitted dates
1cup chopped pecans	2 tablespoons grated orange rind

Syrup:
Heat together 1 cup orange juice, 2 cups sugar, and 3 tablespoons orange rind.

Mix eggs and sugar; beat well and add margarine. Stir in flour, milk, nuts, and dates a little at a time (flour the nuts and dates before adding). Grease and flour a Bundt pan. Pour in batter. Bake at 250°. Turn cake out when done. Poke holes in cake and pour the heated syrup over the cake.

Submitted by Margie Head. Margie served the Hillwood FCE president and the County Council President. She is known for her singing and painting. Margie has done large murals and glass painting.

Orange Frosted Cake
1 box yellow butter cake mix
2 oranges
3 red apples
1½ cups sugar
Prepare 2-layer cake according to box instructions. Allow to cool.

Frosting:
Hand grate 2 oranges and 3 apples (peel and all, but no seeds) and mix with sugar. Frost cake and refrigerate. It is best if allowed to set for 8-10 hours.

Submitted by Wanda Stringer. In honor of her mother Buena Jinnett. This recipe is 100 years old at least. My grandmother would make this at Christmas and served it with boiled custard. It was a favorite of our family.

Mandarin Orange Cake
1 Box Butter Cake Mix
½ cup oil
4 Eggs
1 small can mandarin oranges
Combine all ingredients and bake 30 minutes at 300 degrees in 3 greased and floured cake pans. Let cool.
Icing: 1 Small pkg. vanilla instant pudding
12 oz. carton of Cool-Whip
1 medium can crushed pineapple
Mix together and frost cake. Keep refrigerated.

Submitted by Jane R. Morrison.

Mandarin Orange Cake
1 butter-recipe yellow cake mix
3 tablespoons water
1/3 cup vegetable oil
3 large eggs
1 small can of mandarin oranges with juice
Filling:
12 ounces whipped topping
1 large box vanilla instant pudding
1 can (20 oz.) crushed pineapple in juice
Preheat oven to 350°. Mix together cake mix, oil, water, eggs, oranges, and juice. Place batter into three greased-and-floured round pans. Bake 23-25 minutes or until cake springs back when touched. Mix filling ingredients together by hand and spread between layers and on top and sides of cooled cake.
Keep Refrigerated.

Submitted by Nancy Logue. I moved to Clarksville from Houston, Texas. I am a substitute teacher and have four grandchildren. I enjoy visiting the Smith-Trahern Mansion and bake a cake for the sweetheart cake bake every year.

Mary Jane's Jam Cake
2 sticks margarine
2 cups sugar
3 well-beaten egg yolk
1 cup blackberry jam
3 cups plain flour
½ tsp. salt
1 tsp. soda
1 tsp. cinnamon, nutmeg, allspice
1-cup buttermilk
3 stiff-beaten egg whites
1 tsp. vanilla
Cream margarine and sugar; add egg yolks and jam, beat well. Add sifted dry ingredients alternating with milk, beating well after each addition. Fold in egg whites. Bake in 3 prepared 9-inch, layer pans in 350 degree oven about 30 minutes.

Mocha Chocolate Frosting:
6 tablespoons cocoa
6 tablespoons hot coffee
6 tablespoons butter
1 tsp. vanilla extract
3 cups confectioner's sugar
Dissolve cocoa in coffee, add butter and vanilla extract, and beat until smooth. Add sugar gradually until of spreading consistency.

Submitted by Jacqueline Crouch. This cake defined home and my Mother's love. She made this Christmas treat for me to take and enjoy while away from home over the holidays visiting Ned's parents.

Jam Cake

4 eggs	1 tsp cloves	1 tsp vanilla
1 ½ c sugar	1 tsp cinnamon	1 small apple grated
¾ c shortening	1 10 oz jar of jam	1 cup chopped pecans
2 1/3 cup flour	1 tsp baking soda	½ tsp salt
2/3 cup buttermilk		

Cream sugar and shortening. Add eggs. Beat well and add dry ingredients alternately with milk ending with flour. Pour into 2-9inch cake pans that have been greased and floured. Bake in 350 degrees for 40-45 minutes. Ice with caramel icing or your favorite white icing.

Submitted by Mary Moore. In honor of her mother Mariel Thompson. This recipe is over 100 years old. My mother was a wonderful caring person, an outstanding cook and homemaker. She was a devoted and talented member of the FCE (Home Demonstration Club) since it originated in the 1940's. She left a rich heritage for all to follow and cherish.

Blackberry Jam Cake

1 c. butter, soft	3 tsp. cocoa
2 c. sugar	2 tsp. soda
1 c. blackberry jam, seedless	3 tsp. cinnamon
2 cups buttermilk	3 tsp. allspice
4 cups flour	1 tsp. nutmeg
Nuts as desired	

Mix butter and sugar well, add jam. Add flour and dry ingredients alternately with buttermilk. Mix well and add nuts. Flour and grease tube pan. Bake 250 to 300 degree oven for 2 ½ hours until done.

Submitted by Linda Ellison. Grandmother Browning lived in a coal mining camp in Louellen, Kentucky. She raised 5 children while raising a garden canning her vegetables to help feed her family. She loved to grow flowers. The children remember picking blackberries for this cake.

Grandma's Apple Cake
Mix: ½ cup shortening (or oil)
        1 cup sugar
        2 eggs
Add: 1½ cups flour
        1 tsp. soda
        1 tsp. cinnamon
        ½ tsp salt
Add: 4 to 5 large apples (3 seem plenty)
        1 tbs. vinegar
        1 tbs. water
Bake at 350 degrees 40 to 45 minutes.

Submitted by Debby Johnson. In Honor of Louise Hays Trice Carter. Grandma Carter was my New Providence, Montgomery County anchor when I grew up where the Air Force took Dad. She was a great cook who didn't use recipes much. This is a favorite of my Dad, we have used it many years.

Easy Date Cake

1 cup chopped dates	½ cup shortening
1 cup hot water	1 egg
1 cup sugar	2 cups flour
¼ cup nuts	1 tsp soda

Pour hot water over 1 cup of chopped dates and let stand while you stir sugar, egg and shortening together. Add date mixture and blend well. Add the 2 cups of flour sifted with soda. Add chopped nuts and pour into a greased and floured 9 inch square cake. Bake in a 350 degree oven for 45 minutes. Serve with frosting or whipped cream.

Submitted by Mary Moore. In honor of her mother Mariel Thompson.

Prune Cake
1½ cups sugar
2 cups self-rising flour
¾ cup Wesson oil
1½ tsp baking soda
3 whole eggs
1 tsp nutmeg
1 cup buttermilk
1 tsp allspice
1 tsp vanilla
1 tsp cinnamon
1 cup cooked prunes cooled and chopped
1 cup chopped black walnuts
Sift dry ingredients together. Beat together sugar and oil, add eggs, vanilla and buttermilk. Beat in dry ingredients. Stir in prunes and black walnuts. Pour into greased 9 x 12-inch pan. Bake at 325° for 40 minutes or till done.

Glaze: Mix 1 cup sugar
½ cup buttermilk
1 Tbsp vanilla
1 Tbsp white or dark corn syrup
½ stick butter
Combine in pot and bring to a boil. Boil one minute, remove from heat. Poke or cut holes in hot cake and pour glaze over while still hot. Let set overnight.
Leftovers freeze well.

Submitted by Carolyn Wagner. This recipe has been made in my family for at least 70 years but don't know where it came from. I have to make it every Thanksgiving and Christmas for my brothers. Everyone likes it even if they don't like prunes.

Sweet Potato Cake

2 cups cooked, mashed sweet potatoes	1 ½ cups vegetable oil
2 cups all-purpose flour	2 cups sugar
1 ½ tsp. baking soda	2 tsp. pure vanilla extract
1 tsp. salt	4 large eggs
1 ½ tsp cinnamon	1 cup chopped pecans
1 tsp. nutmeg	½ cup raisins
½ tsp. ground cloves	
¼ tsp. ginger	

Peel, cook, drain, mash sweet potatoes and measure 2 cups. Set aside. Preheat oven to 350 degrees. Grease and flour Bundt pan. Lightly toast nuts in skillet or place nuts in small baking dish and toast for 5-7 minutes. Cool. Combine flour, baking soda, baking powder, salt, cinnamon, nutmeg, cloves, and ginger. Beat the oil and sugar with an electric mixer on medium speed for 1-2 minutes. Add vanilla then the eggs, one at a time, beating well after each addition until the mixture is smooth. Add the sweet potatoes and dry ingredients and beat on low until the batter is smooth. Fold in nuts and raisins. Pour in Bundt pan. Bake approximately one hour or until top springs back when pressed with a finger. Cool in the pan for 20 minutes and invert cake onto a plate and cool.

Praline Frosting

3/4 cup firmly packed brown sugar
6 Tbs. butter
4 ½ Tbsp. milk
1 ½ tsp. vanilla extract
2 cups powdered sugar

Bring brown sugar, butter, and milk to a boil in a 2 qt. saucepan over medium heat, stirring as needed to keep from burning. After it reaches a rolling boil, boil for one minute. Remove from heat; stir in vanilla. Gradually whisk in powdered sugar until smooth. Continue whisking 3 to 5 minutes or until mixture begins to cool and thicken. Pour immediately over cake.

Submitted by Barbara Wilbur. In honor of Sarah Christy Drenthe.

Fruit Cake

1 pound seeded raisins

½ pound lemon peel

1 pound seedless raisins

1 dozen eggs, separated

1 pound pecans

1 pound butter

1 ½ pounds figs

4 cups flour

1 ¼ pounds cherries

2 cups sugar

1 ½ pounds dates

½ cup grape juice

1 ¼ pounds pineapple

3 Tbsp. sorghum

2 tsp. soda

½ pounds orange peel

2 tsp. each cloves, cinnamon, allspice

Dredge fruit in flour until all fruit is dry and separate. Let stand. Stir soda in sorghum. Cream sugar and butter, add fruit along with grape juice, sorghum, and egg yolks (well beaten). Add spices and then well beaten egg whites; blend well. Put cake in greased tube pan. Cork the stem and cover with 2 thicknesses of oil paper and tie securely. Put in pressure cooker and leave petcock open 25 minutes. Close petcock and steam cake 1 hour 15 minutes at 15 pounds of pressure. Then bake in oven for 30 minutes at 200 degrees.

Submitted by Chris Crow. In honor of Lillie Belle Hunter Crow (1917-2004).

Chestnut Sour Cream Coffee Cake
3 cups unbleached flour
1 ½ tsp. baking powder
1 ½ tsp. baking soda
¼ tsp. salt
½ cup unsalted butter (softened)
1 ½ cup sugar
3 eggs
1 Tbsp. vanilla extract
2 cups sour cream
8 oz. chestnut puree (sweetened)
2 oz. mini chocolate chips
Preheat oven to 325 F. Grease Bundt pan, 10 inch tube pan, or two 9 inch loaf pans. Combine the flour, baking soda, baking powder and salt in a medium bowl. With electric hand mixer beat the butter and sugar until fluffy. Add the eggs and beat well. Beat in vanilla and sour cream. Add the flour mixture to the sour cream mixture and mix well. The mixture will be very thick. Remove 1 cup of the mixture to another bowl. Add the chestnut puree and mini chocolate chips and mix well. Spoon 1/2 of the batter into the Bundt pan and top with 1/2 of the chestnut batter. Another layer of vanilla batter, then remaining chestnut batter. Insert a butter knife through the batter layers and swirl once or twice to marble. Bake 60-65 minutes for Bundt pan or 45-50 minutes for loaf pan, until the top of the cake is no longer shiny and tester comes out clean. Cool slightly, remove from pan and dust with a mixture of powdered sugar and cocoa powder. Freezes well.

Submitted by Gabriele Eiseman. The chestnut tree not only provided employment for the people of Appalachia, but gave them the chestnuts for sustenance. They produced chestnut flour and it became known as the "Flour of Appalachia." The chestnut blight, introduced to America in 1904, had destroyed most of the chestnut trees by the 1920's & 30's, creating a double hardship. The Appalachians lost not only their employment, but their bread flour.

Angel Food Cake

12 egg whites
1½ tsp. cream of tartar
¼ tsp. salt
1½ tsp. vanilla
½ tsp. almond extract
Beat until foamy and gradually add:
¾ cup sugar
Beat until it holds stiff peaks
Sift together 4 times and fold into egg white mixture:
1 cup sifted flour
7/8 cup sugar
Pour into ungreased tube pan. Bake 350 degrees 35-45 minutes.
Remove from oven and hang upside down until cool.

Submitted by Katie Smith. Katie has been involved in FCE about 20 years. She enjoys the variety of events and education programs at the mansion. As a Master Gardener, she co-chairs the mansion gardens, incorporating historical aspects into the gardens.

Aunt Lucille's Pound Cake

2 cups sugar	2 cups flour
2 sticks butter	1 Tbs. almond extract
6 eggs	1 Tbs. vanilla

Cream the sugar and butter. Add 2 Tablespoons flour; beat in 1 egg, alternate with flour until all the eggs and flour are used. Add flavoring.
Bake in a greased tube pan at 350 degree oven for 1 hour.

Submitted by Jacqueline Crouch. In honor of her Aunt Lucille. Aunt Lucille was my favorite relative! She was independent, funny, a great confidant, and fabulous cook. Her rolls were divine, her twice-baked potatoes up-town, and this pound cake better than most.

Cherry Cheesecake

8 oz. cream cheese softened
1 can Eagle Brand sweetened condensed milk (14 oz.)
1/3 cup lemon juice
1 tsp. vanilla
1 graham cracker pie crust
1 can cherry pie filling

Beat cream cheese until smooth; gradually add condensed milk and vanilla. Mix in lemon juice. Pour into graham cracker pie crust and chill 3 hours. Top with cherry pie filling before serving.

Submitted by Kanina Davis. In honor of her grandmother Jennie Louise Heflin Smith. Louise, known to her grandchildren as "Granny," was a child of the Great Depression. She was frugal, thrifty and a consummate saver. She however, was generous with her family and loved to cook for her church homecomings and family holidays. She will always be remembered by her family as a woman with a comedic sense of humor who loved to dance and could tear it up on the piano with her rendition of "Down Yonder."

Chess Cake

1 package 2-layer butter recipe cake mix
½ C melted margarine   4 eggs
8 oz softened cream cheese   1-pound confectioner's sugar
1 teaspoon vanilla

Combine cake mix, margarine, and 1 egg in bowl and mix well. Press into 9 x 13-inch cake pan. Combine remaining 3 eggs, cream cheese, confectioner's sugar and vanilla in bowl and beat until creamy. Pour into prepared pan. Bake at 350 degrees for 35 minutes or until lightly browned.

Submitted by Hillwood FCE. In honor of Frances Hatcher. Frances and her sister Marie Cross were the first African American members of Hillwood. They were invited to visit by Martha Pile, who attended their family reunion.

Sweets & Desserts

Clarksville Children's Parade 2016
First Place Entry
Theme "Super Heroes"

Tennessee Triumph Cook Book

Old Fashioned Fudge

1 stick of butter or margarine	1 c milk (evaporated)
2 Tbsp cocoa	1 tsp vanilla
2 c sugar	½ c nuts (optional)

Combine dry ingredients first. Add milk, butter, and vanilla. Cook in large iron skillet for approximately seven minutes. Remove from heat. Beat until smooth and thick. Pour into greased pan and let cool.

Submitted by Shirley Winn. In memory of her grandmother Nancy Oneda Wooten Griffy (1897-1974). Oneda Griffy was dedicated to taking care of her husband and 10 children. My father said she only went to town once each year and that was to buy Christmas gifts for the family. She made delicious desserts for those sugar-loving Griffys.

Double Chocolate Fudge

1 can (17oz) sweetened condensed milk
2 cups semi-sweet chocolate chips
10 oz. unsweetened chocolate
1½ cups of chopped nuts (optional)
1 tsp. vanilla

Line an 8x8x2 inch baking pan with aluminum foil. Butter the foil. Stir milk and chocolate chips in a 2-quart casserole; add chocolate. Microwave on 100% power about 1 minute, stir. Microwave until mixture can be stirred smooth, about 2 minutes longer. Stir in vanilla and nuts spread mixture evenly in pan. Refrigerate until firm. Cut into squares. Makes about 2 pounds of fudge.

Submitted by Nancye Britton. Nancye is a member of Hillwood FCE club, where she has served as club president as well as past County Council President. She enjoys cooking and always bakes for the Sweetheart Cake Bake. Nancye is an enthusiastic member on the board of the Roxy Theater.

Suzy's Caramel Pecan Bars
1½ - 2 cups chopped pecans
12 to 16 whole graham crackers
1 cup brown sugar
¾ cup butter
2 Tbs. whipping cream
1 tsp. pure vanilla
(I double the filling ingredients or do 1½ measures)
Bake pecans 10 minutes or until toasted, stirring halfway through.
Line a cookie sheet or jelly roll pan with non-stick foil. Arrange
graham crackers in a single layer on foil. They may overlap a little.
Combine sugar, butter, and cream in a saucepan; bring to a boil over
medium heat, stirring often.
Remove from heat, stir in vanilla and pecans.
Pour mixture over graham crackers, spreading to coat all crackers.
Bake at 350 degrees for 10 to 11 minutes.
Cool completely and cut into bars.

Submitted by Suella Arrington.

Caramel Fudge Squares
Combine 1 lb. box brown sugar and ½ cup white sugar with 1 cup
melted and cooled butter.
Add 4 eggs one at a time and beat well after each addition.
Stir in 2 cup flour sifted with 1 tsp. baking powder, pinch of salt and 1
tsp. vanilla.
Pour into buttered 8" x 16" pan. Bake at 300° for 45 minutes. Cut
into squares, roll in powdered sugar. Will be chewy.

Submitted by Hillwood Club. In honor of Mary Fern Bradley, a retired
teacher who joined Hillwood.

Toffee

| 2 sticks margarine | 1 cup white sugar |
| 2 (2 oz) bars of milk chocolate | ¼ cup nuts (optional) |

In a sauce pan heat margarine and sugar to boiling point. Let simmer until caramel colored (15 to 20 minutes). Pour onto cookie sheet and spread. Break up chocolate and sprinkle over the toffee, mix in slightly with the tip of a knife. Sprinkle with nuts and allow to cool. Break into 2 inch pieces of crumble to be used in ice cream.

Submitted by Hillwood FCE. In honor of Elaine Harrison (from Mary Hahn). After FCL training, Elaine ran for City Council. She moved to Illinois.

Banana Pudding

1¾ cup sweet milk
4 egg yolks
1 Tbsp. Butter
1½ cup sugar
2 tbs. flour
1 tsp. vanilla
5 bananas, sliced
Box of vanilla wafers

Scald milk in top of double boiler, beat egg yolks. Add sugar and flour. Mix well. Add a small amount of milk to egg mixture. Slowly add to milk stirring until thickened. Remove from stove and stir in butter and vanilla. Let cool, stirring occasionally. Place vanilla wafers in bottom of bowl to cover. Layer sliced bananas and small amount of custard. Continue to do so alternating wafers, bananas and custard.

Meringue: 3 egg whites   ¼ cup of sugar

Beat egg whites until stiff, gradually adding sugar. When it peaks spread on top of pudding. Brown in a 350 degree oven.

Submitted by Mary Moore. In honor of her mother Mariel Thompson. This recipe was put in Tennessee Homecoming Cookbook. Mariel said, "Always make it for those you love." She often did.

Evelyn's Banana Pudding
½ cup self-rising flour
½ tsp pure vanilla
1 cup sugar
3 bananas sliced
3 eggs separated
1 box vanilla wafers
3 cups milk
Mix flour, sugar, milk, and beaten egg yolks. Put in double boiler and cook until smooth and thick. Line casserole dish with vanilla wafers, cover with sliced bananas, and then cover with pudding. Repeat.
Meringue: 3 egg whites, ½ cups sugar, ¼ tsp .vanilla. Beat egg whites until stiff, slowly add sugar and vanilla. Beat until firm. Spread over pudding, bake 350 degrees until browned

Submitted by Artie Terrell. In honor of Evelyn Terrell. Evelyn was a positive and creative influence on her family, Hilldale Baptist Church, Community, and youth and adults. She was an organizer, author, friend, and best companion. She was a Charter Member of Belmont FCE (then Home Demonstration Club). She was a great friend and supporter of Smith Trahern Mansion.

Banana Pudding
2 boxes instant vanilla pudding
1 (8oz) sour cream
3 cups milk
1 box vanilla wafers
1 large cool whip (thawed)
6 large bananas
Gently fold first four ingredients together. Layer wafers, bananas and pudding mixture. Sprinkle crushed wafers on top refrigerate.

Submitted by Nancye Britton.

Rice Pudding

First: 1 cup rice   Second: 2 cups milk
     Quart boiling water   2 eggs beaten
     Pinch of salt   1 tsp. vanilla
                                     ¼ to ¾ cup sugar

Wash rice thoroughly in cold water, stir while adding rice to boiling water. Cook until done, about 20 minutes. Drain, rinse with cold water. Drain well. Mix 2nd part, add rice, put into buttered baking dish. Set in pan with a little hot water. Bake at 300° for 30 minutes.

Submitted by Debby Johnson. In honor of Alice Marie Batson (Ingram). Alice Marie became "Mimy" when Deborah Kathryn Trice was trying to call her grandmother. She volunteered at Salvation Army, sewed for charities, and was a friend to all her neighbors. I remember eating cornbread and milk in a green glass with Dandaddy, my grandfather, and having fun being with them.

Puddin' Cake and Sauce

1 cup butter   2 cup sugar
3 eggs   1 cup milk or buttermilk
2 cups self-rising flour   1 Tbs. Vanilla or lemon flavoring

Cream butter and sugar together. Add eggs. Mix well. Add sifted flour alternately with milk. Mix well. Add flavoring. Bake in a large sheet pan at 350 degrees for 30 – 35 minutes.

Sauce:

1 cup sugar   1 tbs. flour
2 cups milk   1 tsp vanilla or lemon flavoring

Bring to a boil, stirring often. Do not allow to boil over. Cook 10-15 minutes more. Serve over the pudding cake. Serve warm.

Submitted by Willie Mae Miller. In honor of her mother Ms. Drucilla Garrett. Growing up on a farm most of the ingredients we used came from products Mom and Dad raised on the farm. We made our own butter and the flour came from Ringgold Mill. Of course we had to get our sugar from the grocery. My family enjoyed this recipe very much.

Berries and Cream Pie

¾ cup sugar	1/3 cup flour or 3 tbs. cornstarch
2 tbs. butter	¼ tsp. salt
2 cups milk	1 teaspoon vanilla
3 slightly beaten egg yolks	9 inch pastry shell

Sliced strawberries or berries to line pastry shell and cover top of pie
In saucepan, combine sugar, flour, and salt. Gradually stir in milk. Cook and stir over medium heat until bubbly. Cook and stir 2 more minutes. Remove from heat. Stir small amount of hot mixture into yolks; immediately return to hot mixture. Cook for 2 minutes, stirring constantly. Remove from heat. Add butter and vanilla. Line pastry shell with berries; add filling, then cover top berries.

Submitted by Jane Arrington. In honor of her mother Mary Arrington. Mary was a fabulous cook. Whenever she contributed pies to bake sales, her husband, John K. Arrington, would show up and buy her pies to take back home to enjoy. At church suppers, he always chose her pie for dessert.

No Bake Pumpkin Pie with Gingersnap Crust

Filling:	**Gingersnap Crust:**
1 pkg. 3.4 oz vanilla instant pudding	1 c. crushed gingersnaps
1 pkg. 3.4 oz butterscotch instant pudding	½ cup melted butter
1 c evaporated milk	
1 can pumpkin (16 oz)	
1/2 tsp. each of cinnamon, ginger, cloves	
3 c whipped cream	

For crust, mix snaps and butter and press into pie plate. Bake 20 minutes at 350 degrees. In a bowl add pudding mixes to milk. Blend and add pumpkin and spices. Fold in 2 cups whipped cream. Pour into gingersnap crust and let set in freezer. Before serving, garnish with remaining 1 cup whipped cream.

Submitted by Barbara Brown Beeman. Barbara won 2nd place in Leaf Chronicle contest with this recipe.

Sweet Potato Pie

3 large eggs

Dash of salt

½ stick butter

3 cup cooked mashed sweet potatoes

1 unbaked 9-inch pie shell

¾ cup sugar

¼ Tbsp nutmeg

1 cup heavy cream

Beat eggs. Mix sugar and butter well. Add eggs to sugar and butter mixture. Add cream and sweet potatoes. Mix thoroughly. Add nutmeg and pour in pie shell. Bake in preheated oven 350 degrees for 1 hour.

Submitted by Hillwood FCE. In honor of Carrie Rudolph. Carrie Rudolph was Sevella Terry's mother (Clarksville's beloved Jimmy Terry's Mother-In-Law) and a member of Hillwood FCE Club.

Sweet Potato Pie

2 cups mashed sweet potatoes

4 Tbs. Butter

¾ cup sugar

1 tsp. cinnamon

½ tsp. allspice or nutmeg

2 eggs

1 cup milk

½ tsp. vanilla

Beat the potatoes with mixer until very smooth. Add butter, sugar, and spices to hot mashed potatoes. Beat eggs and add milk and vanilla. Add to potato mixture. Pour in unbaked pie shell. Bake at 375° for 50 minutes to 1 hour. Serve with whipped cream if desired. Submitted by Doris Fairrow. We had a large family and this is one of our mother's favorite recipes. Most of the time she used it as a casserole instead of a pie. It was just as good.

Oatmeal Pie
¾ cup sugar
6 Tbs. butter
2 eggs
2/3 cup brown sugar
2/3 cup oats
Cream sugar and butter, add well beaten eggs. Stir in remaining ingredients and pour into unbaked pie shell. Bake 325 degrees for 40-45 minutes. Makes 1 pie.

Submitted by Pat Woods. Pat is the creator of "Eyes Up Forks Down" etiquette and leadership training. She teaches 8 to 80 and loves the art of the home through Sango FCE.

Pecan Pie
3 eggs slightly beaten
1 cup of Karo syrup (light or dark)
1 cup of sugar
2 T oleo melted
1 t of vanilla
1 ½ cup pecans
1 unbaked pie shell
In large bowl combine first five ingredients until well blended. Stir in pecans. Pour into pie shell. Bake at 350 degrees 50 to 55 minutes.

Submitted by Kanina Davis. In honor of her Aunt Rose. Rose Lewis Roe was born in Indian Mound, Tennessee into a large farm family. Rose went to work as a teller at the Northern Bank of Tennessee becoming the first woman to be named as a branch manager. She was a lifelong Methodist who served her church in both word and deed. She was an avid bridge player and loved to entertain. Above all things she loved her family, most especially her grandsons David and John.

Golden Pecan Pie
¾ cup sugar
1 tablespoon all-purpose flour
Pinch of salt
3 eggs, well beaten
1 cup light corn syrup
1 teaspoon vanilla extract
2 tablespoons butter or margarine softened
1 cup pecan halves
1 unbaked 9-inch pastry shell
Combine dry ingredients in large mixing bowl. Add eggs, syrup,
vanilla and butter.
Beat with electric mixer until blended. Stir in pecans and pour
mixture into pastry shell. Bake at 350° for 55 to 60 minutes.

Submitted by Brenda Harper. In honor of my grandmother Martha
Foster Hutchison. Everything Mattie Hutchison cooked was great.
She was probably proudest of her pecan pie recipe because Southern
Living printed it in their magazine and included it in their annual
cookbook.

Chess Pie

1 ¼ cup of white sugar	1 tsp. meal
3 eggs beaten	1 stick of butter
1 teaspoon vinegar	1 tsp. vanilla flavor

Mix all of the above ingredients together. Bake in 350 degree oven
for 30 or 35 minutes.

Submitted by Willie Marie Kilgore. In honor of her mother Emma
Killebrew. Willie Marie is the oldest daughter of John and Emma
Killebrew. Former president of Rossview Home Demonstration Club,
Emma was married to John Killebrew Sr. and mother of 12 children.
She was an active member of New Hope Missionary Baptist Church.

Chess Pie

Cream together:	Add:
½ stick butter	1 tsp. vinegar
1 cup sugar	pinch of salt
½ cup brown sugar	1 Tbs. vanilla
2 Tbs. corn Meal	

Add 3 whole eggs and beat barely enough to mix. Overbeating will cause filling to separate. Cook slowly about 40 minutes.

Submitted by Chris Crow. In honor of his mother Lillie Belle Hunter Crow (1917-2004) from her mother Alice Ann Osborn Hunter (1880-1972).

Bumblebee's Fudge Pie

Melt 1½ sticks butter	Add 1½ cup sugar
1/3 cup whole wheat flour	8 T cocoa (about ¾ cup)

3 eggs, one at a time, beating thoroughly
Pour into buttered 10" pie plate; sprinkle generously with pecans.
Bake at 350° for 20-30 minutes until tester inserted comes out clean.
Cool, serve with ice cream or whipped cream. 8 servings

Submitted by Barbara Brown Beeman

Ginger Krinkles

2/3 cup Wesson oil	2 tsp, soda
1 cup white sugar	½ tsp. salt
1 egg	2 tsp. cinnamon
4 tbsp. Molasses	1 tsp. ginger
2 cups sifted flour	

Heat oven to 350 degrees. Mix first 4 ingredients and then the dry ingredients. Drop 1 tsp. of batter into the sugar and place on ungreased cookie sheet. Oven rack about medium. Yield 4 dozen.

Submitted by Grace Soloman. Grace Soloman was a quiet and gracious woman who was a member of Potpourri Home Demonstration Club.

Dutch Apple Cobbler
Pastry for 1-crust pie

Filling:	Topping:
1 cup sugar	1 cup rolled oats
2 Tbsp. flour	1/3 cup flour
½ tsp. cinnamon	½ cup brown sugar
6 cups peeled, sliced apples	½ tsp. cinnamon
¼ tsp. nutmeg	¼ tsp. salt
1/8 tsp. ginger	1/3 cup butter

Roll pastry. Line inside of 8 or 9-inch pie pan. Mix filling ingredients. Put into unbaked crust. Rub topping ingredients together with fingers. Sprinkle over filling. Bake at 375° degrees for about 1 hour.

Submitted by Leslie Henson.

Apple Crisp
Peel 6 apples and slice. Place in a greased dish and sprinkle with 1 tsp cinnamon and ½ cup of water.
Mix ¾ cup sugar, ½ cup flour and cut in 6 Tbsp. margarine. Sprinkle on top of the apples. Bake in 400° oven for ¾ hour or less.

Submitted by: Jacqueline Crouch. This is a favorite recipes given to me by Ned's mother shortly after we married. It is a family favorite.

Tea Cakes

½ cup Butter	½ cup Sugar
1 tsp. Vanilla	1 egg yolk
1 cup flour	

Cream butter and sugar, blend in egg yolk and other ingredients. Roll into little balls and place on ungreased cookie sheet. Bake 375 degrees for 12 minutes.

Submitted by Ann Wentz. My mom, Mrs. Drucilla Garrett, was a great homemaker who spent a lot of time in her kitchen. She loved her husband and 9 children. She taught us how to love God and each other.

Hello Dollies

1 can coconut (approx. 1 cup)
1 stick butter, melted
1 cup graham cracker crumbs
1 cup semi-sweet chocolate chips
1 can sweetened condensed milk
½ to 1 cup chopped pecan

Melt butter in a greased 8x8 pan. Press crumbs on top. Layer remaining ingredients and bake for 30 minutes at 325 degrees. Cool in refrigerator. Cut into squares to serve.

Submitted: by Pat Woods for Ann Lindsey. My mother Ann Lindsey was a real "fire cracker" and my best friend. Her cooking was straight forward---each meal was a meat, a starch, and a vegetable---but Hello Dollies were her go to cookie when she was in a rush.

No Bake Rum Balls

32 Vanilla Wafers   1 cup pecans
2 Tablespoons cocoa   ¼ cup white corn syrup
¼ cup dark rum or capful or two of rum flavoring*
Confectioner's sugar

Use blender or food processor to process vanilla wafers (in batches) into a fine crumb. Empty into mixing bowl. Process the pecans into a fine crumb and add to vanilla wafers. Add cocoa, syrup, and rum. Mix well. Coat hands with confectioner's sugar and roll the mixture into ½" balls. You can reroll balls in the sugar. Refrigerate for one hour before serving. Yield: 4 dozen. *If you don't have a bottle of rum, buy two bottles of the 'airplane size' bottles of rum.

Submitted by Pat Woods. Pat serves as treasurer of Montgomery County FCE and staffs the Smith Trahern Mansion. As a military wife, her spouse retired here and they chose to stay in Clarksville.

Rum Balls

8 oz. vanilla wafers crushed	2 T butter
1 cup chopped nuts	½ cup corn syrup
1 pkg chocolate chips	1 t. rum flavoring

Combine all ingredients and form into 1" balls.
Roll in powdered sugar.

Submitted by Hillwood Club. In honor of Eileen Branch Hillwood member who opened her own daycare.

Chocolate Chip Cookies

1 ½ sticks of butter (she used margarine) melted
½ pkg. dark brown sugar
¾ cup white sugar
2 tsp. vanilla
1 ¾ cup plain flour
¾ tsp. salt
¾ tsp. baking soda
1-½ eggs (well beaten)
½ bag chocolate chip bits
Around 13 Tbsp of water

Mix flour, salt, soda together in a bowl. Mix butter and sugar very well, add the vanilla, when smooth add flour and alternate with a spoon of water. Add the chips. Use a small spoon to measure each cookie and put on a buttered cookie sheet- these will spread so place them about two inches apart. Set oven on 325 degrees and bake about 10 minutes. FYI- Nana used a gas oven.

Submitted by Jacqueline Crouch. Nana quoted the recipe from memory. Nana's were golden brown, going toward dark brown, and almost paper thin, crisp and divine! Good luck getting them thin enough.

Turtle Cookies

¾ c butter	2 Tsp evaporated milk
¾ c sifted powdered sugar	¼ tsp salt
1 tsp vanilla	

Blend well the 5 ingredients. Blend 2 cups sifted plain flour. Chill dough for one hour. Divide the dough; roll half at a time on floured surface and cut into round cookies about the size of a half a dollar. Place cookies on ungreased cookie sheet and bake at 325 degrees for 12 to 15 minutes or until lightly browned. Remove cookies and cool. Spread each cookie with caramel filling, chocolate icing, and pecan topping.

Caramel Filling – Combine in top of double boiler, ½ pound Kraft light colored caramels and ¼ cup evaporated milk. Heat until caramels melt, stirring often. Remove from heat and stir in ¼ cup butter, 1 cup powdered sugar and 1 cup of pecans finely chopped. Spread while hot.

Chocolate Icing – Melt 1 (6 oz) package of semisweet morsels with 1/3 cup evaporated milk over low heat in double boiler. Remove from heat: stir in 2 tablespoons butter, 1 teaspoon vanilla and ½ cup sifted powdered sugar. Spread over caramels while the chocolate is hot. Cover with pecan half.

Pecan topping – 1 teaspoon caramel filling, ½ teaspoon chocolate icing and 1 pecan half.

Submitted by Shirley Winn. In memory of her grandmother Pauline Morrow Martin (1904-1991. Pauline Martin was a great reader. I got my love of books from her when I was very young. She encouraged her daughter and granddaughters to stand up for their beliefs.

Roasted Almond Thumbprints

1½ Cups all-purpose flour
1½ cups unsalted, roasted almonds
1 teaspoon baking powder
½ teaspoon kosher salt
1 cup (2 sticks) unsalted butter room temp
½ cup granulated sugar
1 large egg
1 teaspoon vanilla extract
½ cup coarse sanding or raw sugar
Jams and/or lemon curd (for filling)

Place racks in lower and upper thirds of oven; preheat to 375°.
Pulse flour and almonds in a food processor until almonds are very finely ground. Add baking powder and salt, pulse to blend.
Using an electric mixer on high speed beat butter and sugar until light and fluffy, about 4 minutes. Add egg and vanilla and beat until pale and fluffy, about 4 minutes. Reduce speed to low and gradually add dry ingredients; mix just to combine.
Place sanding sugar in a shallow bowl. Scoop out dough by the tablespoonful and roll into balls (if dough is still sticky, chill 20 minutes). Roll in sugar and place on 2 parchment lined baking sheets, spacing 2" apart. Using your thumbs, making a deep indention into each ball. (For more exaggerated cracks, bake dough 5 minutes before indenting.)
Bake cookies, rotating baking sheets halfway through, until golden, 12-14 minutes. Transfer to wire racks and let cool. Fill with jam or curd (use a small spoon).
Make ahead: Cookies can be filled 2 weeks ahead; wrap tightly and freeze. Thaw before filling. Cookies can be filled 1 day ahead; store airtight at room temperature. Makes about 4 dozen.

Submitted by Hillwood FCE in honor of Carol Stichal. Carol, a health conscious gourmet cook who thought shopping at the grocery store for the best of fruits and supplies was fun.

"Good Cookies"

¾ cup butter	1 cup sugar
1 cup brown sugar	2 eggs
2 ½ tsp. vanilla	4 cups of Bisquick

In a large bowl cream butter and sugars until smooth and light. Whip together the 2 eggs and vanilla and stir into the creamed mixture. Add 4 cups of Bisquick, blend well. At this point, you can divide the recipe into 2 batches. Add ¾ cup peanut butter into half of the mixture and a 12 oz. bag of chocolate chips into the other half. Or make one kind of cookie. Refrigerate mixture (s) until well chilled. Drop by teaspoonful 2 inches apart on a lightly greased cookie sheet (you can press down lightly with a fork). Bake 350 degrees 15 minutes.

Submitted by Pat Woods. In honor of her Aunt Rose Lindner. My Aunt Rose was not blood but she was family. She and my mother Ann Lindsey were best friends (like sisters) for more than 40 years. Rose was a great "scratch" cook and my mother and Aunt Rose loved to exchange recipes.

Chocolate Malted Strawberry Ice Cream

You can make any amount, but the larger the better and you keep it in the freezer. Never lasts long.

Ingredients: 1/2 gal Whole Berry Strawberry Ice Cream
Malted Milk Ball Candy-12 oz. Box

Directions: When you get home from the grocery store your ice cream may be a little softer. This is the time to take the malted milk balls and but in a plastic bag and crunch (a variety of size pieces is best). Mix into the ice cream. Put in a freezer safe container and refreeze.

Submitted by Martha M. Pile. Martha learned to make this late one night thanks to Barbara Unruh at our Bethlehem UMC Women's Retreat. We found a $ store. There was none left the next morning.

Other

Katie Smith making no baked apples by boiling the apples in small amount of water and red hot candy until apples become rather opaque. Can be made the day before the event and refrigerated or add marshmallows centers and broil until marshmallows are golden brown. This was a recipe was shared as a Holiday Leader Training by then UT Extension Agent Martha Pile and was often demonstrated at the Smith Trahern Mansion (Home of Family and Community Education) for the beauty of the dish and for the ease of preparation.

Martha's Mansion Sorbet

1 pk. lemonade mix (Kool-Aid)
1 can sweetened condensed milk
5 oz paper cups
Directions:

Make up lemonade mix as directed. Stir in one can of condensed milk. Mix all ingredients together until well blended. Put paper cups on small tray and pour mixture into cups and put in freezer. Take out of freezer 5-10 minutes before time to serve. Take each cup and squeeze sorbet out in to dessert dish. Top each serving with two blueberries and a bit of mint.

Submitted by Martha Pile. Martha serves this at mansion dinners, between the main course and dessert, to clean the palate. Guests often complain, "Oh, I wanted a piece of those gorgeous cakes for dessert!" Martha worked as UT Extension Consumer Science Advisor for 42 years, created the Smith Trahern Mansion, and serves as mansion advisor.

Ripe Tomato Ketchup (or Ripe Tomato Chili Sauce)

1 gallon ripe tomatoes	2 cups sugar
2 cups cider vinegar	6 large green peppers (chopped)
4 large onions (chopped)	2 Tbs. Kosher salt
1½ tsp. cinnamon	1½ tsp. dry mustard
2 cans tomato paste	

Scald and peel tomatoes, cut into quarters, then into eights. Cook tomatoes, onions, peppers, and other seasonings, uncovered until they are tender and the juices are thickened through evaporation. Add the 2 cans of tomato paste and continue to cook until thickened. Watch closely at this point, stirring frequently. Pour hot sauce into clean pint jars and seal. No processing required. (Today's safety standards require processing in a hot water bath 15 minutes.)

Submitted by Chris Crow. In honor of Lillie Bell Hunter Crow (1917-2004) from her mother Alice Osborn Hunter (1880-1972).

Sweet Pickles

7 lb. sliced cucumbers
1 gal water
1 box alum
1 qt dry lime
1½ lbs. pickling salt
2 quarts apple cider vinegar
½ box mixed spices
5 lbs. sugar

Slice cucumbers and put in 1 qt lime and 1 gal cold water. Let set 15 hours.

Wash and drain. Then soak in 1 gal salt water 4 hours. Wash and drain.

Soak in clear water 2 hours.

Take 1 box alum and 1 gal water. Add cucumbers and bring to a boil. Drain and wash in cold water.

Bring pickles, sugar, spices and vinegar to a boil. Let simmer for 30 minutes. Turn off heat and let cool overnight.

Next day pack pickles in jars. Strain spice from vinegar mixture. Bring mixture to a boil. Pour over pickles in jars and seal. (Today's safety standards require water bath 10 minutes.)

Submitted by Shirley Winn. In memory of her mother Margaret Martin Griffy (1928 – 2014). Margaret was a wonderful mother and excellent cook. She worked full time until retirement and always believed women should participate in voting. She definitely had an opinion on most things.

Party Tips

Plan your party! You can't start planning the day of the party. Time, money, equipment and space all come into play. What kind of party do you want to give? Did you know when you give a party, you give a gift to family and friends. But that does not mean it has to be expensive or over the top.

As the hostess/host you set the tone. As the hostess, it's your job to make everyone feel welcome, comfortable and relaxed. If you are in a panic when your guests arrive they will feel like they are in the way and an inconvenience.

Wear something comfortable and relax! Everything does not have to be perfect. *Clean the rooms the guests will use.* Prepare the bathroom, make sure it is clean. Check the 'sneaky places': under the toilet seat, the tub, and under the sink. Make sure there is plenty of hand soap, towels (paper is fine too) and toilet paper.

Don't experiment on your guests! Make dishes that are your 'tried and true dishes'. If they are coming for a 'tasting' then they should be prepared to be surprised. The less adventurous may still want to stick to the old stand-by such as chips and dips.

Mix and match your table, use the things you've been collecting for years. These may start a conversation!

Use foliage instead of flowers for arrangements and/or fruits and vegetables. *Unscented* candles are best where there is food served.

Splurge on nice linen and "put your money on the table." The look and feel of quality linen can make the most down to earth food look delicious and bountiful.

Use place cards for a seated meal. You can buy them or make them yourself. (Hint: This is a good project for children).

The more guests you have the warmer it will be inside – adjust the thermostat.

Don't run out of ice. Have more on hand than you think you'll need especially if your party is outdoors.
Put ice in inexpensive Styrofoam coolers. Store unopened bags of ice in the tub.

Spills happen, so have stain removing supplies and old towels handy.

Remember it's your party too! Have fun, make memories, pamper your guests a little (not too much or they may not want to leave).

Entertaining - focuses on material things
Hospitality - focuses on people

Patricia A. Woods, Etiquette Consultant
Excerpts taken from *Entertaining with Style* By: Michele M. Atkins, Extension Director, Henry County

One Dozen Rules for the Table

Do keep elbows off the table

Do chew with your mouth closed

Do put your napkin in your lap, fold it in half if it is very large

Do place the napkin to the left side of the plate if you leave the table

Do swallow your food before you take a drink

Do blot your mouth before you take a drink

Don't hold your utensils like a shovel

Don't blow on hot food

Don't push food onto your fork with your fingers

Don't lick your fingers

Don't reach. Ask for the item to be passed to you. The salt & pepper shakers are always passed together

Don't place a utensil onto the table after it has been used

Pat Woods, Etiquette Consultant

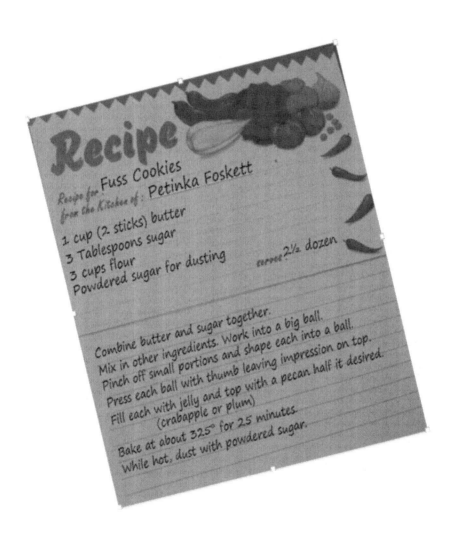

Recipe

Recipe for: Fuss Cookies
from the Kitchen of: Petinka Foskett

1 cup (2 sticks) butter
3 Tablespoons sugar
3 cups flour
Powdered sugar for dusting

serves 2½ dozen

Combine butter and sugar together.
Mix in other ingredients. Work into a big ball.
Pinch off small portions and shape each into a ball.
Press each ball with thumb leaving impression on top.
Fill each with jelly and top with a pecan half it desired.
(crabapple or plum)

Bake at about 325° for 25 minutes.
While hot, dust with powdered sugar.

The Fuss Cookie Skit

By Martha Martin Pile, Retired Extension FCS Agent, with special recognition for much assistance from Beverly Guinn.

This story is taken from the article by Charles Waters 1998 "Cumberland Lore," a supplement Historic Section of the Leaf Chronicle.

The recipe in this article was provided by Ruth Langford who was President of Edgefield Home Demonstration Club now fce/Family and Community Education. Ruth and her two sisters Big Sister-Elmira Stephen and Ann Curtis Christian were known as wonderful cooks and great entertainers, loved hosting the fce club and loved the Smith Trahern Mansion.

Recently Carmen Annette Gentry eldest grandchild of "Muh" or Ann (Ann Dent Northington Curtis Christian, daughter of Gale Curtis and Great Niece of Ruth) and Elmira shared that there was a little competition among the sisters dealing with recipes and outdoing each other as well. This family has a great cook book that has many of the Sisters' special recipes and much more. Carmen said when she was around seven years old, she learned much by watching and even helping her Great Aunt Ruth preparing for her clubs and groups.

Note: Petinka Bailey Foskette & Willie Erwin Daniel are on the "Harper List" of suffragists active in Clarksville as is Lou Redd Roach, Mary Dunlop's mother.

ACT I
(Entering Cafeteria in Washington D.C.)

Mr. Foskett: *(Looks around and says)* "Can hardly believe that it is 1940 and I am still at the Internal Revenue Service here in Washington D.C. I am running a little late today."

Doorman: "Sorry, it is still crowded in the cafeteria today."

Mr. Foskett: "Oh, I see and empty chair at the table over there." *(Walks to table.)*

Seated Gentleman: *(Looking over a 1940 D.C. Newspaper)* "May I invite you to join me?"

Mr. Foskett: "Thank you kindly. I am Griffith Foskett-originally from Clarksville, Tennessee."

Gentleman: "This is indeed a strange coincidence. I spent last night in that pretty little city. My, do they have good food in that Southern Town. I am bringing my wife a recipe right here in my pocket that caused a big fuss over 20 years ago."

ACT II

(Home of Petinka Foskett with best friend Mary Roach Dunlop - 1920 wall calendar)

Petinka Foskett: "You are indeed my best friend to stop by and visit before our out of town trip. That Griffith Foskett had to go to the bank. Please come have a seat by me *(pats the empty chair)* and we can just visit for a little while."

Mary Dunlop: "You are also my best friend and such an excellent cook and hostess. Patinka, I was wondering about your name."

Petinka Foskett: "I was born Augusta Gabriella Bailey, but the name was too much for my brother and my sister Lucy Bailey to pronounce. You know my brother C.W. Bailey. Well, Lucy said I was such a cute child and they began calling me "pretty thing." Over time, the name was shortened to "Petinka" and that is what everyone calls me today and surely will till the day I die."

ACT III

(Petinka at her home talking on the phone to Mary at her home)

Petinka *(on the phone):* "Hello Mary, just wanted you to know we have returned home safely from our trip. Guess what, I brought a new recipe with me. It is a very small short bread cookie. But it is special."

Mary: "Please tell me more. Wait, let me get a pencil and paper. All right, please, please give me the recipe. You know I am always on the lookout for new recipes."

Petinka: " No, please… do not ask me for the new cookie recipe Please wait until I serve it in my home, then I will give it to you."

Mary: "Oh, please what can I do to persuade you to share it with me? I promise not to serve it in my home until you have served it to our Home Demonstration Club Meeting."

Petinka: "If you make a solemn promise not to serve it until then. They are called the Thumb Print Cookie, and here is the recipe."

ACT IV

(Social tea at Mrs. W.M. Daniel's house. Utilize audience as guests at the social-BIG HATS)

Petinka: *(speaking to a few of the ladies as she comes in the room)* "Mrs. W. M. Daniel is the grand dame of Clarksville's social set, is she not..... I was so glad that we got home from our trip in time to come.

Woman: "She surely is. She asked Mary Dunlap to help. Everyone is raving over Mary's new cookie recipe."

Mary: *(emerges from the kitchen with a plate of the cookies in her hand and speaking to those around her)* "Thank you...... I am glad you like the cookies ... thank you......" *(Looks up to see Petinka!)*

Petinka: *(temper flares)* "I tell you what Mary Dunlap, you are not my best friend, or a friend at all. Let me tell you what I think of someone that would break a solemn promise. It is very obvious that you had rather be one of Mrs. Daniel's social set, sharing my cookies in the swankest home in Clarksville than be my friend... You can surely forget being my friend."

Other Women: *(Start talking/gossiping among themselves)* ..."Can you believe what she said to her"....Mary Broke her solemn promise, she did".... "Oh, my"..... "I will call you on the telephone as soon as I get home"..."Oh, good, I am on your party line and will listen in"...

ACT V

(Back to the two gentlemen in Washington)

Gentleman: "Can you believe it – Fussing over a cookie recipe? That is the strangest thing, do you not agree?"

Mr. Foskett: "No, the strangest thing I ever heard is that I sat down with you and you are carrying that recipe in your pocket. You see, my wife was one of the women who had that fuss in the first place."

Wins State Championship

With

"Etora Flour"

Miss Sarah Howard
Liberty, Tenn.

LIBERTY GIRLS' HOME DEMONSTRATION CLUB WINNER!

Clarksville, Tenn., Dec. 9, 1922.—(Special)— Because she made the fluffiest, tastiest and most delicate light bread, biscuits, corn and whole wheat muffins in the community, county and six-county contests, Miss Sara Howard, 13-year old daughter of Mr. and Mrs. J. B. Howard, a second-year member of the Liberty Girls' Home Demonstration Club, has spent the past week in Chicago attending with all of her expenses paid, the International Live Stock and Grain Show, from Dec. 2 to 9. Miss Howard won out with a safe score over contestants in the Liberty community contests, and won a score of 95, she took the honors away from five other girls of this county and on Aug. 9, in Columbia, she won first honors with a score of 94 over girls from Giles, Marshall, Bedford, Wilson, Sumner and Montgomery counties.

Miss Howard was accompanied to Milan by Miss Oma Worley, county home demonstration agent of this county. At Milan she joined the party of West Tennessee girls chaperoned on the remainder of the trip by Miss Bertha Corbett, county home demonstration agent of Madison county. Miss Howard and the West Tennessee party were joined at Chicago by East Tennessee club boys and girls.

Montgomery County is justly proud of Miss Howard because of her culinary qualifications. She is not only adept in cooking, but possesses many other admirable qualifications in connection with the household.

About the same time as the Suffrage ratification, County Home Demonstration Clubs were working to bring women valuable knowledge and teaching practical application regarding improved sanitation, hygiene, food safety and so much more. The life-skill lessons they taught enhanced families and communities, helping them thrive. Current Family and Community Educator clubs are their legacy organizations. FCE continues the tradition to support the growth and development of its members, their families and their communities.

The Monday Evening Music Club
Customs House Museum Collection, Gift of Georgie H. Miller